DANTE'S MODERNITY

Cultural Inquiry

EDITED BY CHRISTOPH F. E. HOLZHEY
AND MANUELE GRAGNOLATI

The series 'Cultural Inquiry' is dedicated to exploring how diverse cultures can be brought into fruitful rather than pernicious confrontation. Taking culture in a deliberately broad sense that also includes different discourses and disciplines, it aims to open up spaces of inquiry, experimentation, and intervention. Its emphasis lies in critical reflection and in identifying and highlighting contemporary issues and concerns, even in publications with a historical orientation. Following a decidedly cross-disciplinary approach, it seeks to enact and provoke transfers among the humanities, the natural and social sciences, and the arts. The series includes a plurality of methodologies and approaches, binding them through the tension of mutual confrontation and negotiation rather than through homogenization or exclusion.

Christoph F. E. Holzhey is the founding director of the ICI Berlin Institute for Cultural Inquiry. Manuele Gragnolati is professor of Italian literature at Sorbonne Université in Paris and associate director of the ICI Berlin.

Claude Lefort

DANTE'S MODERNITY
An Introduction to the *Monarchia*

With an Essay by Judith Revel

TRANSLATED FROM THE FRENCH BY
JENNIFER RUSHWORTH

EDITED BY
CHRISTIANE FREY
MANUELE GRAGNOLATI
CHRISTOPH F. E. HOLZHEY
ARND WEDEMEYER

ISBN (Print): 978-3-96558-003-9
ISBN (PDF): 978-3-96558-004-6
ISBN (EPUB): 978-3-96558-005-3
DOI: 10.37050/ci-16

Cultural Inquiry, 16
ISSN (Print): 2627-728X
ISSN (Online): 2627-731X

Bibliographical Information of the German National Library
The German National Library lists this publication in the Deutsche
Nationalbibliografie (German National Bibliography); detailed
bibliographic information is available online at http://dnb.d-nb.de.

Cover design: Studio Bens

In Europe, the paperback edition is printed by Lightning Source UK Ltd.,
Milton Keynes, UK. See the final page for further details.

The digital edition can be downloaded freely at:
https://www.ici-berlin.org/oa/ci-16/.

ICI Berlin Press
An imprint of ICI gemeinnütziges Institut für Cultural Inquiry Berlin gmbH
Christinenstr. 18/19, Haus 8
D-10119 Berlin
publishing@ici-berlin.org
www.ici-berlin.org

Contents

Preface vii
Translator's Note xv
Acknowledgements xix

Dante's Modernity
CLAUDE LEFORT 1

Lefort/Dante: Reading, Misreading, Transforming
JUDITH REVEL 87

References 109
Notes on the Contributors 113

Preface

BY CHRISTIANE FREY

This volume presents for the first time in English translation a lengthy essay on Dante's *Monarchia* — one of the most important, if often overlooked, political treatises of the late medieval period — by the French political philosopher Claude Lefort. The essay was written to appear with a new translation of Dante's text published in 1993 at Lefort's instigation in a book series he edited for the French publisher Belin.[1]

As is already evident from its length, Lefort's essay pursues ambitions that go far beyond its ostensible editorial function as a preface to Dante's treatise. Indeed, many of the texts through which Lefort developed his thought and intervened in public debate took the form of forewords, introductions, prefatory notes, and ancillary essays that appeared in editions and translations of both historical as well as recent works of political philosophy and history — a fact that speaks both to the dialogical character of Lefort's thought and to the central role that *reading* plays in his work.[2] As Judith Revel shows in her essay for this

---

1   Claude Lefort, 'La Modernité de Dante', in Dante, *La Monarchie*, trans. by Michèle Gally (Paris: Belin, 1993), pp. 6–76. The book was reissued by Belin as a paperback in 2010.

2   Among his more substantial ancillary texts are 'Le Nom d'Un', in Étienne de La Boétie, *Le Discours de la servitude volontaire*, ed. by Pierre Léonard, intro. by Miguel Abensour and Marcel Gauchet, accompanying essays by Pierre Clastres and Claude Lefort, with additional texts by Félicité Lamennais, Pierre Leroux, Auguste Vermorel, Gustav Landauer, and Simone Weil (Paris: Payot, 1976), pp. 247–307; 'La Cité des vivants et des morts', in Jules Michelet, *La Cité des vivants et des morts. Préfaces et Introductions* (Paris: Belin, 2002), pp. 5–65; 'Préface', in Alexis de Tocqueville, *Souvenirs*, ed. by Luc Monnier, with notes by J. P. Mayer and B. M. Wicks-Boisson (Paris: Gallimard, 1999), pp. i–l.

volume, 'Lefort/Dante: Reading, Misreading, Transforming', Lefort's exercises in revisiting works of the past are one of his preferred ways of intervening in the present. This is particularly true of the essay on Dante. It presents a highly original interpretation of the *Monarchia* and of its significance for the history of modern politics and political thought, and it allows Lefort further to develop his own political theory while taking it in new directions.

From his critique of the Communist Party's bureaucratization of working-class politics, through his dramatic break with Sartre, the undisputed leader of French post-war intellectual Marxism, to his criticism of the Left's apologetic response to the Polish and Hungarian uprisings in 1956, Claude Lefort established himself early on as a thinker who did not hesitate to criticize the Left from within its own ranks. A major point of contention was the tendency, which Lefort observed in many Marxist thinkers, to posit an overarching theory impervious to the unforeseeable contingencies of historical change. With his signature notion of the 'work of the oeuvre', as developed most notably in his magisterial study of Machiavelli, Lefort insisted on what he saw as the fundamental indeterminacy of the works of the past not as a problem to be overcome, but as a valuable resource with which to counter political dogmatism — to vitiate any claim to have established, once and for all, the truth of the political.[3] Vehement objections of his colleagues on the Left notwithstanding, in the 1970s and 1980s Lefort advanced a defence of democ-

---

3   See Dick Howard, *The Specter of Democracy* (New York: Columbia University Press, 2002), pp. 75–76. Lefort's *thèse d'état* on Machiavelli was directed by Raymond Aron: Claude Lefort, *Le Travail de l'œuvre Machiavel* (Paris: Gallimard, 1972), partially translated into English as *Machiavelli in the Making*, trans. by Michael B. Smith (Evanston, IL: Northwestern University Press, 2012).

racy as a form of open and radical politics while engaging in a sustained analysis and critique of 'totalitarianism', a term others on the Left found unusable. Many of Lefort's most influential writings from this period reflect this development of his thinking, most prominently his critique of bureaucracy and the essays on the political collected in 1986.[4] Another focus of Lefort's work in these years, inspired in part by his continuing engagement with the work of Hannah Arendt, concerned the question of human rights and, more specifically, the possibilities of thinking the 'idea of perpetual peace' in a time in which 'all figures of transcendence have become blurred'.[5] This led Lefort to concern himself — and this is less well known — with the concept of a 'universal empire' that could base itself on a concept of a single humanity,[6] albeit one that would neither rely on the 'old certainties' of exclusive absolute values nor relate merely to circumstantial considerations or 'drift off into utopia'.[7] It was in the context of these considerations that Lefort began to attribute a central im-

---

4   Claude Lefort, *Éléments d'une critique de la bureaucratie* (Geneva: Droz, 1971), a small selection of which is translated and included in Claude Lefort, *The Political Forms of Modern Society: Bureaucracy, Democracy, Totalitarianism*, ed. and intro. by John B. Thompson, trans. by Alan Sheridan, Terry Karten, and John B. Thompson (Cambridge: Polity, 1986), pp. 29–136; Claude Lefort, *Essais sur le politique, xixᵉ–xxᵉ siècles* (Paris: Seuil, 1986), English as *Democracy and Political Theory*, trans. by David Macey (Cambridge: Polity, 1988).

5   Claude Lefort, *Writing: The Political Test*, trans. and ed. by David Ames Curtis (Durham, NC: Duke University Press, 2000), p. 144. English translation of Claude Lefort, *Écrire. À l'épreuve du politique* (Paris: Calmann-Lévy, 1992).

6   On the concept of a 'humanité-une', see, for example, Lefort, 'La Nation élue et le rêve de l'empire universel', in *L'Idée d'humanité. Données et Débats, actes du xxxivᵉ Colloque des intellectuels juifs de la langue française*, ed. by Jean Halpérin and Georges Lévitte (Paris: Albin Michel, 1995), pp. 97–112 (p. 98).

7   Lefort, *Writing*, p. 142.

portance — as he explicitly and repeatedly states himself — to Dante's *Monarchia*.[8]

The three books of Dante's *Monarchia* were written in the second decade of the fourteenth century, and it is still debated whether the treatise was designed to support Emperor Henry VII's campaign to Italy or was composed only after his death in 1313. The condemnation of the treatise by the Church was immediate and long-lasting: burned as heretical by Cardinal Bertrand du Pouget in Bologna in 1329, attacked by the Dominican friar Guido Vernani in his treatise *De reprobatione 'Monarchie' composite a Dante* (written between 1327 and 1334), it was placed on the Vatican's Index of prohibited books in 1554, where it remained until 1881. The *editio princeps* did not appear until 1559 and was printed in protestant Basle.[9] As Lefort shows in his essay, the influence of the *Monarchia* on both the politics and the political thought of the following centuries, while often hidden, could scarcely be disputed. But while the treatise had always been in the focus of theologians, historians, and scholars of Dante, contemporary political science had shown little interest in it, to the point that it was almost unknown to students of political philosophy.

---

8   See, for example, 1981: Claude Lefort, 'The Permanence of the Theologico-Political?', in *Democracy and Political Theory*, pp. 213–55; 1982: 'The Death of Immortality', in *Democracy and Political Theory*, pp. 256–82 and 'The Idea of Humanity and the Project of Universal Peace', in *Writing*, pp. 142–58; 1995: 'La Nation élue'; and 2002: 'La Cité des vivants et des morts'.

9   For a modern English translation see Dante Alighieri, *Monarchy*, ed. and trans. by Prue Shaw (Cambridge: Cambridge University Press, 1996). Shaw is also the editor of the critical Latin edition: Dante Alighieri, *Monarchia*, ed. by Prue Shaw, Edizione Nazionale delle opere di Dante Alighieri a cura della Società Dantesca Italiana, v (Florence: Le Lettere, 2009). Both the Latin text of the *Edizione Nazionale* and Shaw's English translation are now available online: <https://www.danteonline.it/monarchia> [accessed 5 December 2019].

Lefort's choice of the treatise to appear in his book series with Belin was clearly designed in part to remedy this neglect. But in provocatively titling his accompanying essay 'Dante's Modernity', Lefort signalled as well that Dante's treatise was of more than merely historical importance.

The 'modernity' in question is laid out at the outset in a series of claims for Dante's originality: he was the first who thought of humanity as the whole of the human race, the first to imagine a universal society in political terms, and the first to reveal the formative role of force, of wars and division in the advent of such a society. Particularly the third observation begs the question of how we are to understand Lefort's use of the term 'modern'. Is Dante's treatise being measured against a concept of the modern that was already determined in advance? Or is the 'modernity' that Lefort discovers in Dante something that emerges only in the course of his encounter with the text? In the second half of the essay, Lefort patiently pursues the career of Dante's innovations in the political thought and praxis of the succeeding centuries. It is crucial not to confuse these observations with a 'reception history'. Clearly, for Lefort, what is 'new' in Dante cannot be separated from its later avatars — from the varied realizations, distortions, and misapplications it would inspire at later historical junctures. Lefort's method, therefore, presents a direct challenge to prevalent modes of historicization: the work of the oeuvre is not bounded by the moment of its historical emergence, and, however contingent, even errant its fate may be, both interpreters and political reality have to be understood as participating in the unfolding of the work.[10]

---

10   This edition is also motivated by the hope that such a wager will resonate with medievalists in particular, who have long known that the all-too-neat distinction between single-author artefact, canonized at its

Thus, the concept of a single, universal sovereignty that Lefort sees emerging for the first time in Dante takes on a new form and function when it re-emerges in the context of the early modern kingdom, and it is transformed again in the age of the modern nation-state. It is remarkable that Lefort largely abstains from passing judgement on any of these formations. Of the unprecedented efficacy of the *dominus mundi* representation under the conditions of the nation state, for example, we hear merely that it is 'troubling'.[11] One has the impression that, in his probing re-reading of the history of political thought in the wake of Dante, Lefort avoids any appeal, even implicit, to a transhistorical standard of what 'modernity' is or should be. If this is so, then what the essay leaves us with is not just a rethinking of the late medieval poet and political philosopher, but also, and just as importantly, of modernity itself.

This embracing of the present as informed but not determined by the past is characteristic of Lefort's oeuvre as a whole. It is evident here in the way Lefort ends his essay: not by presenting a specific view or interpretation of Dante's innovative idea of sovereignty, but by advocating for the project of 'disentangling' the links between universalism, imperialism, and nationalism that have been instituted in its name. Characteristically for Lefort, the result of this project is left open. As Revel's seminal essay emphasizes, one should not mistake this lack of determinacy regarding any ultimate lesson to be drawn from Dante's

---

inception, and a subsequent and separate 'reception' is a modern and not always helpful construction. For a discussion of Dante's authorship, including the way it is constructed in the *Monarchia*, and its intricate relationship to authority and institutional *auctoritas*, see Albert Russell Ascoli, *Dante and the Making of a Modern Author* (Cambridge: Cambridge University Press, 2008), esp. chapter 5: '"No judgment among equals": Dividing authority in Dante's *Monarchia*', pp. 229–73.

11   In this volume, p. 45.

treatise as a disengagement from present concerns. On the contrary: Lefort's way of doing justice to the modernity of this late-medieval treatise that was often neglected outside the field of Dante studies, as becomes clear through his concluding gesture, is to enjoin his readers to continue the 'work of the oeuvre' his essay traces and models.

Translator's Note

Claude Lefort's essay on Dante's *Monarchia* divides quite neatly into two halves. The first half provides us with an analysis of Dante's text, and comprises an introduction, followed by sections on 'The Human Race', 'Rome and the History of Humanity', and 'The Two Sovereignties'. The second half, more surprisingly, offers an idiosyncratic reception history of the *Monarchia* and its theories, beginning with the fourteenth century ('Dante and Civic Humanism') and moving irregularly through to the nineteenth century, although not entirely in chronological order, since it is back with the sixteenth century that Lefort's essay ends. At a certain point in his essay, Lefort describes the various actors in this process of transmission as 'relays' (*relais*).[1] Extending this image, the whole of Lefort's essay can be said to mobilize two different sets of relays. Firstly, there are the classic works of criticism on the *Monarchia*, with which Lefort is explicitly in dialogue: Étienne Gilson and Ernst Kantorowicz in the first half; Frances Yates in the second. Secondly, there are the political thinkers with whom Lefort engages, some only briefly (Niccolò Machiavelli, Coluccio Salutati, Leonardo Bruni), others more extensively — with the final two sections of his essay devoted, respectively, to Jules Michelet and Étienne de La Boétie.

In a metatextual twist, however, a third set of relays comes to join this already eclectic team. On the one

---

1   Claude Lefort, 'Dante's Modernity', in this volume, pp. 1–85 (pp. 49 and 63). All subsequent page references refer to this translation.

hand, Lefort himself relays Dante's *Monarchia* to a modern French audience through his introduction to a French translation of Dante's text (published in 1993 and 2010). On the other hand, all those involved in the present reworking of Lefort's essay for an anglophone readership must also be credited as additional relays, consolidating Lefort's special place in the reception history of this particular Dantean text. As the translator of Lefort's essay, I would like to record here my debt of thanks to all those who generously contributed to this translation project, both at the conference at the ICI Berlin devoted to Lefort's reading of Dante and in subsequent conversations.[2] In particular, my translation is infinitely better thanks to the painstaking care and patience shown towards it by the four editors, Christiane Frey, Manuele Gragnolati, Christoph Holzhey, and Arnd Wedemeyer. To Lele I also owe special thanks, amongst many reasons for inviting me to collaborate on this project. Last but not least, I am forever grateful to my writing companions Matthew Salisbury and Francesca Southerden.

As someone with a long-standing interest in translation, French theory, and the French reception of medieval Italian authors, it has been a pleasure to spend time with Lefort. Of course, the pleasure has not been without what we might call, borrowing a phrase from Lefort, '*de singulières difficultés*' (a phrase over which we deliberated at surprising length, mostly because of the polysemy of the premodifying adjective: 'singular' in what sense? Merely 'notable' or something closer to 'strange' or 'peculiar'?). Some of these difficulties related to Lefort's prose style.

---

2   'Dante's Political Modernites: Claude Lefort Reads the Monarchia', symposium held at the ICI Berlin on 6 July 2019 <https://doi.org/10. 25620/e190706>.

In this regard, I have taken the decision to break up certain sentences into smaller units, and most of all to add paragraph breaks where feasible to aid the reader in navigating especially long passages. Other difficulties concerned vocabulary, whether that of Dante's *Monarchia* or Lefort's analysis. In confronting the former, Prue Shaw's English translation of the *Monarchia* was an indispensable resource, and it is from that translation that passages from Dante's text quoted by Lefort are also taken.[3] In terms of Lefort's own vocabulary, I relied upon the advice of the editors, although it is worth noting here that some Lefortian phrases remained stubbornly resistant to translation. One such phrase was the heading 'Le travail de l'œuvre', where we eventually opted for 'The Work of the Oeuvre', avoiding the trap of apparent tautology ('The Work of the Work') and taking advantage of the fact that 'oeuvre' in English can also refer to an individual work even if it usually evokes an author's body of works. Finally, I decided to aim to make my translation as gender neutral as possible, and therefore avoided rendering 'homme' as 'man' and 'hommes' as 'men' (save in cases, of course, where the specific gender was intended as such).

When translating Lefort into English, I was struck by the many English and anglophone references in his essay. For example, Lefort devotes a strikingly long section of his essay to the example of Elizabeth I. His reading of Elizabeth I is, moreover, explicitly mediated by the work of Yates,

---

3   Dante Alighieri, *Monarchy*, ed. and trans. by Prue Shaw (Cambridge: Cambridge University Press, 1995). Shaw is also the editor of the critical edition: Dante Alighieri, *Monarchia*, ed. by Prue Shaw, Edizione Nazionale delle opere di Dante Alighieri a cura della Società Dantesca Italiana, v (Florence: Le Lettere, 2009). Both the Latin text of the Edizione Nazionale and Shaw's translation are available online at <https://www.danteonline.it/monarchia> [accessed 5 December 2019].

just as his earlier discussion of Dante's *Monarchia* had been frequently in dialogue with Kantorowicz writing in English (to return to the first of the sets of relays that I mentioned earlier). From this perspective, translating Lefort into English pleasingly means returning some of his references to their original state.

Reading Lefort's essay, I was also struck, as I have already suggested, by the equal weight granted to textual analysis, on the one hand, and the text's reception, on the other. For Lefort, quite simply, 'the oeuvre continues to reveal itself through the work of time' (p. 47). Within this revelatory process, Lefort persuasively makes the bold claim that repudiation is as much a part of reception as adulation, hence the importance of Michelet and La Boétie as prime interlocutors in his narrative. In Lefort's emboldening words (and my translation), 'Whether he inspired praise or refutation, Dante was never forgotten' (p. 43). At the very end of his essay, Lefort tells us that 'in order to examine [Dante's] work', we need to know '*how to use time*' (p. 85). Part of this injunction — which ultimately stems from a passage in *Convivio* IV, ii, 10 — is an invitation to consider time as a crucial factor in forming texts. More personally, however, translation has been for me a matter of knowing how to use time, so that new readers may come to enjoy spending time with Lefort, or more precisely with Lefort and Dante together.

JENNIFER RUSHWORTH

Acknowledgements

The editors would like to express their gratitude to Éditions Belin for granting publication rights for the present translation and to Judith Revel for accepting to engage with Lefort's essay with her usual brilliance and grace. They are particularly grateful to Jennifer Rushworth for her generosity, accuracy, and open spirit in translating both Lefort's and Revel's texts. The editors would also like to thank the participants of the workshop 'Dante's Political Modernities: Claude Lefort Reads the *Monarchia*', held at the ICI Berlin on 6 July 2019, for many valuable insights into Lefort's engagement with Dante. See <https://doi.org/10.25620/e190706>.

Dante's Modernity

CLAUDE LEFORT

As a poet, Dante is universally known and celebrated, his name often invoked alongside the names of Virgil and Homer. Anyone cultured, if called upon to list in limited number the masterpieces of Western literature, could not fail to mention *The Divine Comedy*. Is this glory so dazzling as to have cast a shadow over the figure of the political philosopher, that is, the author of the *Monarchia*? This Dante was without doubt the first to understand the term *humanitas* as both the dignity proper to the human being and the human race taken in its widest sense. He was the first to imagine a universal political society, subject to a single authority whose mission was to reveal to all their citizenship of the same world. He was also the first — unafraid of connecting the advent of the Law to the work of might — to discern the development of universal society as a result of the divisions, wars, or, in his words, 'duels' to which the claimants to the supreme power in turn devoted themselves.[1] How is it, then, that Dante the philosopher

---

1   [Translator's note: Of the word 'duel', Prue Shaw writes that "'Trial by combat" seems the least unsatisfactory rendering of *duellum* in

is only of interest to medieval historians or to theologians, and that students of literature, philosophy, or (as we now say) the human sciences typically reach the end of their education without ever having heard a word about the *Monarchia*, or, if they have, knowing only that this treatise represents one of the last witnesses of the quarrel between Papacy and Empire?

Of course, the circumstances in which the text was written should not be neglected. Dante, we learn, was for a time closely involved in the public affairs of Florence. As a prior he was part of the government of the Commune, and falling victim to the conflict between the two factions which divided the city — the Whites and the Blacks — he had to go into exile after the victory of the latter. Then, being excluded from the amnesty from which most of the Whites benefited, he lost any chance of returning to his homeland. His resentment towards Florence is vehemently expressed in the *Comedy*. According to the most likely hypothesis, he wrote the *Monarchia* in 1311 in the context of Henry VII's descent into Italy with a view to being crowned emperor in Rome. Dante thought that Henry would restore order and that Henry alone would be able to rescue Florence from the formidable control of the Pope. These hopes placed in the purported heir of the Roman Empire were as little founded as those that

---

English': Dante, *Monarchy*, ed. and trans. by Prue Shaw (Cambridge: Cambridge University Press, 1996), p. 53 n. 1. In this matter I follow Shaw's lead subsequently, just as all subsequent citations from the *Monarchia* are taken from Shaw's translation. It should be noted that Shaw is also the editor of the critical Latin edition: Dante Alighieri, *Monarchia*, ed. by Prue Shaw, Edizione Nazionale delle opere di Dante Alighieri a cura della Società Dantesca Italiana, v (Florence: Le Lettere, 2009) and that both the Latin edition of the *Edizione Nazionale* and her English translation are now available online: <https://www.danteonline. it/monarchia> [accessed 5 December 2019].]

Lorenzo de' Medici would later inspire in Machiavelli. In reality, a long time had passed since there had been an Emperor capable of squaring his ambitions with his means. Only Frederick II had briefly shown himself able to build a robustly structured State supported by a legal system which conferred universal authority upon him; and yet, under the title of emperor, he never governed more than the Kingdom of Sicily (which included the south of Italy and Naples). Nonetheless, however accurate we consider this depiction to be, it does not give an idea of the aims which Dante was pursuing in his work. I mentioned Machiavelli: reading him, knowing about the personality of Lorenzo matters little; what the writer portrays, on the occasion of the return of a Medici, is the figure of a *principe nuovo*. Similarly, the illusions which are imputed to Dante tell us little about his philosophical project. Henry VII is a figurehead. Moreover, nowhere in the *Monarchia* is Henry named; only Dante's correspondence reveals who he has in mind. The true name of the emperor is the name of the One.[2]

The *Monarchia* is not a historical document, it is a work, an oeuvre which is extraordinarily innovative, freshly so even after the intervening centuries, in spite of its sometimes arid language and its disconcerting succession of syllogisms. Dante systematically borrows from the writings of important Christian authors, from Saint Augustine to Saint Thomas. He uses the learning of the latter as a rampart against the assaults of the many canonists working for the Papacy, but he does so in order to cause a breach in

---

2   [Translator's note: Lefort poignantly capitalizes crucial terms in ways that are not always predictable. The translation faithfully reproduces these capitalizations. Following other translations and secondary literature, 'le nom d'Un' is translated throughout as 'the name of the One' rather than as 'the name of One'.]

theology, a breach through which human beings escape the omnipotence of the Church and even that of religion. Dante leaves to the priest the task of guiding souls in the quest for heavenly beatitude. Yet human beings, created by God and freed from dogma, are recognizably able to follow their own aims and to attain earthly happiness, the sign of which is spiritual peace for each individual, and universal peace for the human race.

Likewise, Dante places himself under the authority of pagan writers and takes advantage of the jurists who, themselves nourished by the teaching of Aristotle and Roman law, elaborated the conception of a political community as a totality in which all the parts are subordinated to the same aim, ruled by the principles of Reason and Justice. Yet again he does this in order to create, following his own inspiration, the idea of the human race as one *civilitas* (let us not be afraid to translate this as civil society). In the *Monarchia*, then, we witness two types of borrowing and two forms of rupture, in order to open up a new path. Étienne Gilson sheds light on Dante's intentions as follows:

> The only universal community of which the idea existed at the time was a community essentially supernatural and religious: the Church, or, if one prefers, Christendom. Not only had the Church never thought that there should or could exist a Humanity unified for the purpose of pursuing a temporal happiness regarded as its special goal, but it had, since Augustine's *City of God*, discountenanced the ideal of a unification of all mankind through the common acceptance of the Christian faith and under the supreme government of the Pope. In order, then, to conceive of the possibility of a universal temporal community, it was necessary to borrow from the Church its ideal of a universal Christendom and to secularize it. On the other hand, it was impossible to secularize this ideal

> without establishing philosophy as the basis of the
> universal community of all mankind, subject to the
> same monarch and pursuing the same form of hap-
> piness in obedience to the same laws.[3]

It is necessary to stress this point further: the *Monarchia* represents neither a synthesis between Christian and pagan thought, nor even merely the imbrication of the concepts of two traditions in the service of the legitimization of the Emperor. 'Secularizing the ideal of a universal Christendom' means abandoning the precept of humanity's irremediable fallenness; both the individual and the whole of humankind are invested with spiritual power. Dante does more than recover the value of earthly life; he discovers in this life a plan which surpasses and transfigures the mortal condition. Thomas Aquinas, a committed reader of Aristotle, had already spoken, as Gilson reminds us, of 'the necessity which requires humans to communize the resources of their individual reason'[4] and — attentive to the question of the best form of governance — he thought that a political society governed by *one alone* was the most appropriate model for ensuring the cooperation of human beings granted reason for their survival. But, besides the fact that he thought only of the government of a king, he assigned strict limits to such a figure. It is thus an immense step that Dante takes in bestowing philosophical meaning on political life. As Gilson notes, such a step requires Dante to adopt the Aristotelian concept of the *possible intellect*.[5] By this term it must be understood that humans are able to gain knowledge of intelligible matters

---

3   Étienne Gilson, *Dante the Philosopher*, trans. by David Moore (London: Sheed & Ward, 1948), p. 166.

4   Ibid. [translation amended].

5   Ibid., p. 167.

on the basis of the first principles of Reason imprinted within them. Discursive knowledge consequently places humans beneath angels, in whom being and knowledge are the same, but allows them to orientate themselves towards a goal which is proper to them, namely the perfection of their mortal state.

Nonetheless, Dante gives to this concept of the possible intellect an entirely new meaning. While, on the one hand, its operations are still attributed to the human being taken as an individual — the dignity attributed to both philosopher and emperor leaves no room for doubt on this point —, on the other hand its realization requires the participation of all humankind, understood in the full extension of space and time. Dante thus also takes an immense step beyond the field of ancient philosophy. Aristotle conceived of the ideal city as a restricted community, situated in a clearly defined space, so that its members would know each other, either directly or indirectly, with their closeness making it possible to organize their relations correctly. Dante gives up the idea of the limits of natural sociability; the civil society of the human race includes nations of different sizes, peoples who do not know each other, who are exposed to different climates and attached to their particular customs, and whose unity rests on their common submission to the jurisdiction of a monarch. For Aristotle, it was unlikely, though not impossible, that the ideal constitution could become a reality; it depended on chance, which is to say on an extraordinary convergence of events not reliant on human will alone. For Dante, universal *civilitas* shows itself in the course of history; the sign of its advent can be seen in the time of Augustus, and its definitive institution depends on human will. Consequently, a new relationship between philosophy and politics emerges. Although Dante still declares that the contemplative life is superior to the active life, he suggests that they are intimately connected, since the principles of philosophy are imprinted in the order of the world.

The essay that Ernst Kantorowicz dedicates to the *Monarchia* in *The King's Two Bodies* contains a very valuable warning. This learned and astute critic mentions two difficulties 'that no one should think can be passed over lightly'.[6] In short, on every page Dante shows himself to be so dependent on the knowledge and language of his time that the reader can easily overlook the 'slant so new and so surprising' that he gives to all the statements that he has borrowed and miss his intention and the new solutions that he offers.[7] In one sense, this difficulty is indeed overwhelming. But, on reflection, we should be less concerned about failing to grasp the full extent of his borrowings — through lack of the competences of the historian or the theologian — or of the use he makes of the debates about the relations between religion and philosophy. For in this case our confidence in the vigour of his thought, or, to use an image dear to Dante, its fecundity, is only

---

6   [Translator's note: I have not been able to locate the phrase which Lefort presents as a quotation from Kantorowicz — 'dont nul ne devrait croire qu'il pût venir à bout' — in either the English text or its French translation, despite Lefort's references to both. What Lefort seems to offer here is a summary of similar statements about the difficulty of analysing Dante's work made by Kantorowicz at the start of his chapter on the *Monarchia*: especially, the insights that 'Dante, of course, cannot easily be labelled at all' and that 'every Dante interpretation is bound to be fragmentary where Dante himself is complex', as well as the recognition that 'the Dante expositor will be tempted far too often to read into Dante things which Dante neither said nor meant to say'. See 'Man-Centered Kingship: Dante', in Ernst H. Kantorowicz, *The King's Two Bodies: A Study in Mediaeval Political Theology* (Princeton, NJ: Princeton University Press, 1997), pp. 451–95 (pp. 451–53). Lefort's subsequent citations from Kantorowicz are, in contrast, accurate.]

7   Kantorowicz, *The King's Two Bodies*, pp. 452–53.

increased. Moreover, the search for the coherence of the work leads to another risk, that of forgetting that 'The visions of Dante the poet seem to interfere constantly with the logical arguments of Dante the political philosopher'.[8] In essence, Kantorowicz tells us that there is nothing linear in his work; what we find, instead, is a network of correspondences between different themes which borrow from different areas of knowledge. Undoubtedly, the exploration of such a complex oeuvre is beyond our reach. And yet, if it is true that the *Monarchia* eludes an analysis that would seek to reveal the totality of its articulations, does it not also encourage an examination of the development of its thoughts through the variety of its means of expression, its combination of images, stories, and inflexible demonstrations in the form of syllogisms, and its quotations from the Bible and classical texts?

THE HUMAN RACE

The treatise appears to follow a rigorous structure. At the start of the second section of Book I, Dante defines the temporal monarchy known as Empire and announces the three questions he intends to answer and which will be treated in each of the three books: whether this monarchy is necessary for the good of the world; whether the Roman people rightfully claimed for themselves the office of the monarchy; whether the authority of the monarch depends on God directly or on another, a minister or vicar of God (I, ii, 3). But how can we prepare ourselves to follow Dante through the twists and turns of his argument, if we have not first taken the measure of his undertaking? In the theatre where the fate of these questions is

---

8   Ibid., p. 453.

to be decided, Dante places a number of protagonists: namely, Christ and Caesar Augustus, Moses, Aristotle, Virgil, and Thomas Aquinas, the Pope, the Emperor, earlier claimants to the supreme power, and Rome. He lets the Bible and philosophy speak, but he puts himself on stage first and foremost. This fact can even less be overlooked since, throughout the treatise, the persistence of his presence makes itself felt in the repeated use of the first person and in the exercise of a singular voice. Of course, this voice protects itself through the authority of writing or by finding its guarantee in bearing witness to facts, yet it still assumes the burden of proof or of condemnation both of error and of deceit.

Hence, Book I opens with a sort of prologue (I, i, 1–6). Dante places himself among those 'men whom the Higher Nature has endowed with a love of truth' (I, i, 1). This group comprises those — as Dante demonstrated in the *Convivio* — who deserve to be called noble, in contrast to those who have inherited titles from their ancestors or from their wealth. Those enamoured with truth have quite a different notion of what they inherit and what they pass on. They benefit from the work of the ancients who have *enriched* them, and it is their duty to *enrich* posterity in their own turn. From the ancients they received *public* instruction and their concern is precisely with matters of *public* interest. Hence, right at the outset, there is the sense of a shared, unifying purpose bringing generations together, necessitating human cooperation across time in the service of a quest for truth, for a common good. The novelty of this argument should not be underestimated. In one breath Dante acknowledges his debt towards those who have passed their knowledge on to him and his debt towards those who will need his own knowledge in the future. Then, evoking the image — taken from one of the psalms — of "a tree planted by the rivers of water, that bringeth forth his fruit in due season",[9] he suggests that his thoughts have ripened at the appropriate hour. Had he not already stated in the *Convivio* that 'we must consider how it is appropriate to wait for the right time in all our activities and especially in speech', shortly thereafter adding that 'timing must be taken into account, for both speaker and listener'?[10] To be sure, in the *Convivio* Dante is commenting on his own poems; in the *Monarchia*, by contrast, we can assume he is thinking instead of the present time of the world. His intention is not only to stigmatize those who merely devour what they learn (likely an allusion to the intellectual servility of the theologians); rather, he wants to discover 'truths that have not been attempted by others' (I, i, 3). To the sterility of those who do nothing but regurgitate the lessons of the ancients, he opposes the desire to innovate, for it is useless to repeat the words of Euclid, Aristotle, or Cicero. Now, this last statement makes fully evident the extent of what humanism will owe to Dante's audacity. The message is that studying great thinkers and respecting their authority goes hand in hand with the de-

---

9   Dante, *Monarchy*, I, i, 2. [Translator's note: Shaw cites from the Bible in the Authorized Version [AV], save in cases 'Where the English of the AV does not correspond to the Latin quoted by Dante, or blurs the development of his argument, or cannot be accommodated syntactically' ('Editor's note', in *Monarchy*, pp. xxxv–xxxvii (p. xxxvi)). The original of this quotation of Psalm 1, v. 3 has 'his season' rather than 'due season'.]

10   Dante, *Convivio*, IV, ii, 5 and 8. The discussion of the nature of nobility is found in Book IV, especially IV, vii, 9 and IV, viii, 9 (and, on the Emperor's inability to grant nobility, IV, x, 16). [Translator's note: Dante Alighieri, *Convivio: A Dual-Language Critical Edition*, ed. and trans. by Andrew Frisardi (Cambridge: Cambridge University Press, 2018), p. 221. All subsequent translations from the *Convivio* are taken from this edition.]

sire to find in them a call to create new works. Imitation is thus based on the principle of non-repetition. What is here being formulated, I believe for the first time, is nothing less than the modern idea of the oeuvre. The end of the prologue is also remarkable. By declaring that he wants to bring to light the truth of the universal Monarchy, all the while pointing out once more that no one before him had discovered it, Dante announces his hope of winning, for his own glory, first prize in such a great contest. That the treatise should include a *disputatio* is hardly surprising, but the stakes of the confrontation are presented in such a way that the reader will later lend credence to the analogy between Dante's position in the intellectual arena and Rome's position in the arena of the world.

It is thus at the end of this prologue that Dante defines 'Temporal monarchy, then, which men call "empire"' as 'a single sovereign authority set over all others in time, that is to say over all authorities which operate in those things and over those things which are measured by time' (I, ii, 2). Then he states his three questions. Before answering them, however, he takes care to explain their origin. Humans have the ability to think speculatively, to penetrate the knowledge of intelligible beings which do not depend on their power — namely, mathematics, physics, and divine matters —, but they also have the ability to turn their speculative thoughts towards action, to reason about matters over which their will does have power. In essence: the questions which Dante raises belong to the domain of political philosophy, the aim of which is to establish the principle of legitimate constitutions. Political philosophy does not attempt to determine the purpose of this or that particular society, but rather the ultimate end of life in society, bearing in mind that this ultimate purpose merges with the first cause of this life, which is the cause of everything, that is, the cause of all human actions. Hence, we find Dante abruptly declaring:

> whatever constitutes the purpose of the civil society of the human race [...] will be here the first principle, in terms of which all subsequent propositions to be proved will be demonstrated with sufficient rigour; for it would be foolish to suppose that there is one purpose for this society and another for that, and not a common purpose for all of them. (I, ii, 8 [translation amended])

In these few lines, the break with Aristotle is accomplished, producing a reformulation of the opposition between the *particular* and the *universal*. But for Dante, who is certainly aware of Aristotle's intention, it is important that this break remain implicit. To be sure, the author of the *Politics* does not, in fact, conceive of an end which would be specific to each type of society; as we saw, he is fully convinced that life in society derives from a single principle, that, consequently, there exists a constitution true to nature and reason (which are one and the same). However, that is the extent of this constitution's universality; it can only be realized in the space of the city. Dante introduces the idea of a new kind of universality: the end or the universal cause belongs to humanity understood as the whole of humankind.

In short, the exploration of the question already reveals the answer. Nonetheless, though the answer may be indicated, it still calls for an explanation of why humanity contains in itself its own end, while being part of a much larger whole, and why it must be led by *one alone*. Let us first consider two arguments, both of which draw on Aristotle. The first relies on the metaphor of the body: nature produces the thumb for one end, the hand for another, the arm for yet another, and, finally, it is for an entirely different end that the whole being is created. The political body is conceived according to the same model; the individual, the family, the town, the city, and the kingdom all have their own specific ends, and all these ends are subordinate to the end for which the human race was created (I, iii, 1–2). Making use of the phrase 'nature does nothing in vain' (God being here conflated with Nature), Dante points out that things are defined not by their essence but by what they do. Thus it seems that there is an activity that cannot be imputed to any of the particular bodies, and that alone is universal, and belongs to humanity. Ostensibly remaining within the framework of classical philosophy, but not hesitating to transgress its doctrine, Dante recalls that humans differ from animals not only in their sensitivity to things with which they come into contact, but also in their ability to conceive of these things through the *possible intellect,* in order to conclude that the ultimate end of humanity is the intellective power or virtue. It is at this point that Dante puts forward the following extraordinary proposition:

> And since that potentiality cannot be fully actualized all at once in any one individual or in any one of the particular social groupings [...], there must needs be a vast number of individual people in the human race, through whom the whole of this potentiality can be actualized. (I, iii, 8)

Despite the reference to Averroes at this point, it is clear that the possible intellect does not refer to a substance which is separate from the body. But this observation, which I take from Gilson, is not sufficient.[11] The intellect

---

11   Gilson, *Dante the Philosopher,* pp. 169–71.

does seem to have a relation with the body of humanity, a body composed of many members which coexist while also succeeding each other in time. Of course, Dante does not state this explicitly, but it must surely be understood that speculation and speculation with a view to action — philosophy and political philosophy — are involved in the condition of the human race and caught up in its history. Dante, let us note in passing, immediately signals that by the term *intellective power* he understands the speculative intellect and the practical intellect which is but an extension of the former. At this point ought we not to remember his prologue? If he could set his sights on the discovery of truths heretofore entirely unknown, was this not because he knew how to take advantage of the support of classical thinkers and also how to draw on new resources in the present state of the world?

The first argument can be presented summarily. Suffice it to indicate that the lengthy considerations concerning the analogy of the whole and the part, the relationships of the parts to one another, then the supremacy of the whole, and, finally, the necessity of one principle governing the whole, lead to the conclusion that the human race requires a single monarch. In the course of these considerations emerges the important theme of universal peace (which will accompany that of unity until the end). The second argument is based on the authority of the Bible. It is summed up in the following few lines:

> It is God's intention that every created thing should show forth His likeness in so far as its own nature can receive it. For this reason it is said: 'Let us make man in our image, after our likeness'; for although 'in our image' cannot be said of things lower than man, 'after our likeness' can be said of anything, since the whole universe is simply an imprint of

divine goodness. So mankind is in a good (indeed, ideal) state when, to the extent that its nature allows, it resembles God. But mankind most closely resembles God when it is most a unity, since the true measure of unity is in him alone; and for this reason it is written: 'Hear, o Israel, the Lord thy God is one.' But mankind is most a unity when it is drawn together to form a single entity, and this can only come about when it is ruled as one whole by one ruler, as is self-evident. (I, viii, 2–4)

The way in which Dante here interprets the teaching of the Bible is no less *new and surprising*, to return to Kantorowicz's terms, than his treatment of the teaching of Aristotle. The human being as God's creature is equated with humanity. The idea of humanity is no longer supported by the image of the political body — family, village, city, kingdom — as understood by the philosopher, but rather by the image of Adam's body. Reasoning based on the analogy of the part with the whole or on the subordination of the part to the whole is replaced by the mystical identification of the human race with man understood in his first perfection. Although already present previously, the thought of *the one* proves to be more profound than that of the whole. Likewise, the function of the monarch no longer stems as much from the need for a principle governing the whole and for an agent able to render this principle effective, as from the need for a body the sight of which assures humankind of its own form and identity.

This brief examination of the first two arguments reveals much about the way in which Dante proceeds. Kantorowicz said that there was nothing linear in Dante's thought; in fact, he follows a path which he then abandons once he has reached his goal. When the answer to a question seems to have been given, he starts out on a new path in the direction of the same goal. The first route contains signs which point to the second exploration, while traces of the former remain discernible in the latter. In order to establish that the world is in the best possible condition when it experiences peace and concord under the authority of *one alone*, Dante relies first on philosophy and then on Scriptures; he places reason as the first principle, and then divine will. Witnessing this approach, we are tempted to ask what is meant by the new bifurcation demonstrated by his considerations about judgement. In effect, without any transition, he declares that wherever there is disagreement, there must there also be judgement (I, x, 1). The change in direction is at first glance even more surprising than the preceding one. Summarized succinctly, his third argument will be as follows: two lords who are in disagreement need to call upon a third party, of a higher jurisdiction, in order to resolve their differences. However, if this third party has only limited authority, their decision risks being contested by another who has equal powers of jurisdiction. Thus recourse to a new third party proves necessary, and the process would be endless were there not a sovereign judge against whom none can be opposed. Whence the need for a universal monarch, for a third party who is absolutely *other*.

This reasoning seems to follow a formal logic. However, it proceeds from an idea which remains implicit: divisions between people are not brute divisions resulting from their natural separation and which, in this sense, have no other outcome than war and the domination of the weak by the strong. In a dispute, each party is in fact within its rights in asserting itself, and wants to have these rights recognized. Thus the requirements for there to be a universal monarch ensue from the fact that every indi vidual, regardless of motives, has an idea of right. Let us be in no doubt that the reference to Aristotle at the end of the passage mentioned (I, x, 6) has no other purpose than to persuade us that the path taken coincides with that of philosophy. At this point, it is worth noting that the words attributed to Aristotle referred, in the *Politics* (IV, 4), to a verse from Homer, the meaning of which appeared to Aristotle unclear: 'No good thing is a multitude of lords' (*Iliad*, II, v. 204).[12] Dante, rather than evoking Homer, refers to Virgil. It is Virgil who is credited with having shown that the world is in its best state when justice rules over it. Dante cites from the *Bucolics* the following verse, well known at the time: '"Now the Virgin returns, the reign of Saturn returns"', explaining that Virgil addressed Justice as the Virgin, also named Astraea, and that the reign of Saturn indicated the golden age (I, xi, 1). For centuries, Christian authors had favoured Virgil, either because they saw in him a poet who, despite his paganism, evinced the highest moral virtues, or because they interpreted his poems in an allegorical manner, more specifically finding in the *Fourth Eclogue* a sign of the coming of Christ on earth.[13] Dante is therefore no more innovative in calling upon Virgil than in invoking Aristotle. However, it is necessary to consider that here a new authority does appear,

---

12 [Translator's note: citing here from Homer, *Iliad*, ed. and trans. by A. T. Murray, rev. by William F. Wyatt, 2 vols, Loeb Classical Library, 170 (Cambridge, MA: Harvard University Press, 1999), I, p. 77.]

13 'Virgile philosophe et prophète', in Henri de Lubac, *Exégèse médiévale: les quatre sens de l'Écriture*, 2 vols in 4 (Paris: Aubier, 1959–64), II.2, pp. 233–62. This chapter provides important information about interpretations of Virgil since the sixth century, notably with regard to the fate of the *Fourth Eclogue* and to the verse cited by Dante. [Translator's note: the last volume of this work has yet to be translated into English, although for the earlier volumes see Henri de Lubac, *Medieval Exegesis: The Four Senses of Scripture*, trans. by Mark Sebanc and E. M. Macierowski, 3 vols (Grand Rapids, MI: Eerdmans, 1998–2009).]

following the authority of Aristotle and of Christ (or of the Evangelists), and that this new authority enables Dante to introduce a new principle, in concert with Reason and Revelation: Justice. Having understood Dante's intention, we are no longer in any doubt that his considerations about disputes and judgement are undertaken in order to reach the same goal by another route. In effect, it is not so much the demonstration of the necessity of a sovereign judge which now seems to be most important, but rather the relationship established between the ideas of justice and of omnipotence, heralded by the reunion of Astraea and the Emperor.

Of justice it is said both that it is immaterial (an unchanging essence which, like whiteness, knows no difference of degree, or else a divinity, such as Astraea) and that it radiates through the souls of mortals, who are susceptible of receiving this light to a greater or lesser degree, depending on the extent to which they are blinded by their covetousness and able to exert their own will. Now, what man is freed from his desires and capable of allowing himself to be wholly animated by justice, so that nothing in his soul can hinder it? This man is quite evidently someone who has no rival and therefore no reason to be envious. And this man exists; it is the Emperor. In this manner, the reasoning has been reversed. The necessity of a universal monarch is no longer based on the demand of those who seek a judge above them and, in the end, above everyone. Instead, this necessity comes, if I dare put it like this, from on high, from a transcendent justice which requires, in order to be passed on to humans, a minister or vicar who can be, by virtue of his position, completely free of animosity. Moreover, the question whether there exists a lord capable of imposing his decrees is once more answered in the affirmative, namely that he is the one who, beyond the borders of cities and kingdoms, possesses a power of commandment which none can oppose: the Emperor.

Although the demonstration is developed on Virgil's authority, it is probable that the *Bucolics* are not Dante's only source of inspiration. He may have been guided in part by the work of Frederick II's jurists. It is known that a veritable cult of Justice, combined with that of the Emperor, was established under Frederick's reign. The *Liber augustalis* formulated a theory of juridico-centric royalty. Most notably, it declared that by virtue of the *Lex regia*, the *Quirites* had:

> conferred on the Roman Prince both the right to legislate and the *imperium* [...]. Provision, therefore, was made for reasons of utility and necessity [...] that there concur in the selfsame person the origin as well as the protection of Justice, lest Vigor be failing Justice, and Justice, Vigor.[14]

However, assuming that Dante made use of this conception, it must be admitted that he deduces from it consequences that are quite extreme:

> where there is nothing which can be coveted, it is impossible for greed to exist, for emotions cannot exist where their objects have been destroyed. But there is nothing the monarch *could* covet, for his jurisdiction is bounded only by the ocean. (I, xi, 11–12)

The manner in which he develops his apology of omnipotence, by invoking Aristotle and proliferating syllogisms,

---

14 Kantorowicz, *The King's Two Bodies*, pp. 98–99, citing from a section on 'Frederick the Second', pp. 97–143.

is no less remarkable. He returns to the author of the *Nicomachean Ethics* in order to establish the thesis that the being who is most perfect is the most whole and to reformulate the idea of the unity of the human race by turning to the idea of the unity of wills (I, xv, 1–5).

Yet it is more important to notice the use that Dante makes of Scriptures. Already, in a passage where he takes care to explain that the exercise of omnipotence does not entail uniform legislation, the example of Moses is invoked. It was to him that judgements of a higher order concerning all the children of Israel were entrusted; however, he entrusted lower-order judgements to the heads of the tribes, in other words the initiative to apply the law in the particular context of their community (I, xiv, 9). But it is in the last part of Book I that Dante draws from the circumstances surrounding the birth of Christ the ultimate proof of the legitimacy of the Empire:

> All the arguments advanced so far are confirmed by a remarkable historical fact: namely the state of humanity which the Son of God either awaited, or himself chose to bring about, when he was on the point of becoming man for the salvation of mankind. For if we review the ages and the dispositions of men from the fall of our first parents (which was the turning-point at which we went astray), we shall not find that there ever was peace throughout the world except under the immortal Augustus, when a perfect monarchy existed. (I, xvi, 1)

What Dante wants to express is not wholly explicit in this passage. Admittedly, he already calls Augustus a *divine monarch* and sees in the apparition of the Son of God under Augustus's reign a sign of the latter's glory. However, it is not until the end of Book II that his intention becomes fully clear. At that point, he leaves no doubt as to Christ's choice to be born 'under an edict emanating from Roman authority, so that the Son of God made man might be enrolled as a man in that unique census of the human race' (II, x, 6). The edict was therefore just, and Augustus was the agent of God, when, through his census, he made manifest that all mortal beings belong to one same community. Dante goes so far as to maintain that Adam's sin would not have been punished in Christ had the empire not been founded in all due right. He even derives an argument from the fact that the judgement was made not by Herod, a mere king, but by Pilate, an imperial vicar. Doubtless, others before Dante had associated the coming of Christ with the universal census, but he truly seems to transgress the boundaries of the tradition by attributing a sacred mission to Caesar and absolute legitimacy to the Empire.

ROME AND THE HISTORY OF HUMANITY

I have just mentioned the concept of legitimacy. As will be recalled, the first question concerning the necessity of the monarch for the good of humankind was to be followed by a second question concerning the legitimacy of the Roman emperor. Can the two questions be separated? Does the answer to the first not resolve the second? Probably, but it seems that Dante's aim at this point is to show that the history of Rome bears witness to its vocation to include all people and that, as a consequence, whoever appears as its heir holds the legitimacy whose principle was previously established. In committing to this approach, Dante again shows how innovative he is, and it is surprising that critics as insightful as Gilson and Kantorowicz show little interest in Book II.

In fact, Dante audaciously combines the interpretation of the signs which confirm the nobility of Rome (its genealogy, the virtues of its assemblies and citizens) with the interpretation of the signs which confirm its chosen status (the miraculous events which allowed it to escape destruction). This twofold reading of the history of Rome teaches not that right belongs to the most powerful, but that it is *revealed* in the work of might. Moreover, the divisions between people, cities, and kingdoms, which we had learnt are the cause of humanity's misfortune, appear in a new light. These divisions have become empty, but it is through their effect that the human race has achieved unity. Let us note in passing that once more Dante distances himself from Aristotle's teaching. According to the *Politics*, a well-ordered city cannot have conquest as its aim; the care that it affords to its military organization results only from the need to resist an eventual attacker or to discourage any thoughts of aggression. It is, for example, for this reason that the principal vice of Sparta is visible in the essential part accorded in its education to learning skills of weaponry. In contrast, Dante believes that conflict between powers seeking to establish their supremacy, providing that it obeys the rules of honour, as in trial by combat, concerns the fate of humanity. Thus rivalries which appeared a little earlier as contrary to the workings of Justice acquire new meaning. In the past, these rivalries had a beneficial function, as they served the establishment of peace and concord, albeit unbeknownst to those involved. Right has gradually triumphed over the desire for power. Such is the argument that a distinction is outlined between subjective and objective right. What confers legitimacy on the victor is not their intentions, but the result of their action, as they will appear in retrospect to have taken a step forward in the path followed by humanity towards its ultimate aim.

Dante does not overturn his first argument: wherever there is disagreement, a judge is necessary, he argued, then a higher judge, then another still higher, unless there is a monarch above whom there is no one. Rather, this argument finds itself confirmed in the reading of history. Conflicts between claimants to the Empire similarly required the advent of a sovereign judge, who finally appears with the figure of Rome. Dante thus finds a new way to bring out from the shadows where it was hidden the truth of the universal Monarchy. Everyone had been made blind, and, he notes, he himself had been momentarily blinded, by the dazzle of weapons, while what was needed was to discover what was at stake in the coming of justice and reason. At this point, we are once more reminded of his prologue. Dante, as I was remarking, embarks on a campaign against his adversaries: supporters of the Papacy, as Book III will demonstrate. Again we need to ask ourselves whether, by announcing his hope of winning the prize in such an important contest, he is not seeking to prevail over the Philosopher whose heir he claims to be. Whatever the case, Dante's ambition cannot be underestimated. Nor the fact that he puts forward a principle on which the modern philosophy of history will be founded. The idea of a relationship between right and might which is only able to be deciphered upon examination of the events, and of a final state in which the entire meaning of the past is revealed, will return with certain nineteenth-century thinkers. The anticipation even of the theory of the *cunning of Reason* can hardly be doubted, since the interpretation of the major events of the past entails the discovery of a meaning which is written in reverse.

Yet it is true that this interpretation is accompanied throughout by explicit recourse to theology. While he brings the register of a purely human history to the fore, Dante asserts that we must nonetheless read in the succession of key events which marks this history the traces of God's intention. From the start of the Book (II, ii, 4), he declares that 'right is willed by God'. Consequently, considering whether something has been accomplished by right means also *considering whether it is accomplished by God.* Only ignorance and sin are the work of human beings; it is enough for many events to be unworthy of our interest. Just as Reason is not discernible in the detail of facts, and it must suffice to grasp the sequence of conflicts where what matters is supreme power, so likewise are the designs of Providence hidden, yet its intervention cannot be doubted, considering the happy *dénouement* which results from the gathering of all people under the authority of a single monarch.

Let us return to the role attributed to Rome in this second Book. Rome appears as the agent that gives sense to the whole of history. Rome is the nation which has accomplished the promise contained in the struggles for world domination. Rome's success marks, in a way, a sort of end of History, since the divisions of the princes are no longer a factor of right and reason, and, in a way, the start of History, since humanity is now able to know its proper task, even if it hesitates before its accomplishment. Listening to Dante, it would seem that in order for the world to live in peace, it is sufficient for people to recognize the figure of sovereign authority in the one who bears the name of Emperor, successor of Caesar. Nothing in his treatise suggests that war remains necessary in order to assert the Emperor's rights. Dante knows, however, the turbulence of the world in which he lives. His silence regarding the means of restoring the power of the emperor stems from his interpretation of history: war no longer makes sense. A simple *yes* to that which is would be the salvation of the peoples. In other words, Rome is the chosen nation and its heir forever benefits from this choice, since nobody can undo what God has ordained.

Why was it legitimate for the Roman people to assume the office of the Monarchy? This is the question which was announced at the start of the work. The exploration that this question calls for is no less extensive in the second Book than in the first. Effectively, we had understood the principle of the response, but it is worth noting that the answer is given in two different moments. In the second part of the text, Rome is presented as the last protagonist of the drama, as the one who was victorious in the final trial and who has reached the goal of sovereignty over all mortals. Quite extraordinary is the scene in which Dante deploys the pretenders to the Empire: Ninus, king of the Assyrians; Vesoges, king of Egypt; Cyrus, king of the Persians; then Xerxes, son of Darius; finally Alexander, king of Macedonia. All these were unable to win the competition up until the appearance of Rome who, in trial by combat, eliminated the Albans, the Sabines, the Samnites, the Greeks, and the Carthaginians. Each time, the disagreement was resolved by the sword. And right was victorious, as is demonstrated, in the conclusion that we have already mentioned, in Christ's choice to take the form of man during the reign of Augustus.

But the catalogue of Rome's virtues, to which the first part of the text is devoted, seems to me no less worthy of attention. Dante invokes Rome's nobility, taking care to recall that, according to the teaching of the Philosopher, '"nobility is virtue and ancient wealth"' (II, iii, 4). In this way Dante prepares his readers to receive the legend of the foundation of Rome, without letting them forget that the greatness of its ancestors is only to Rome's credit because their descendants were able to preserve the traces of this greatness. He notes that ancestral and personal nobility are not the same thing. The distinction is, indeed, important, and in the *Convivio* Dante had devoted to it a lengthy discussion which makes it impossible to doubt his opposition to aristocratic ethics; a man's dignity has nothing to do with his ancestry, for virtue is not passed on through nature. It is equally impossible to think that it is in the emperor's power to confer nobility on any of his subjects (*Convivio* IV, ix, 16). We must therefore be careful not to mistake Dante's intentions in the *Monarchia*. This supporter of empire sees people through the eyes of a citizen of Florence, that is, of a commune which managed to destroy the power of nobles, and this in combats in which he himself participated. Doubtless, Dante is conservative, in the sense that he defends the prerogatives of Florentines of ancient lineage and is opposed to the political rise to power of immigrants coming from the *Contado*. Thus he feels free to borrow the story of the *Aeneid* without any risk of suspicion. In any case, at this point he is still only following tradition. His apology of Roman citizens will be quite different in import. However, obedient to a pattern which is by now familiar to the reader, Dante interrupts his discussion of nobility in order to introduce a theological argument, all the while juxtaposing Aristotle, Virgil, Lucan, and Saint Thomas. Under the authority of this last, he declares that 'whatever is brought to full realization with the aid of miracles is willed by God, and consequently comes about by right' (II, iv, 1). At this point, the signs of a providential history of Rome appear: the shield that fell from heaven in the time of Numa; the intervention of the goose in the Capitol; the hailstorm which put the Carthaginians to flight; the flight of Cloelia during the siege of Porsenna. All these examples prove that the Roman Empire moving towards its perfection was supported by the attestation of miracles (II, iv, 4–11).

Having proved as much in brief, the author shows, at length, why it was Rome's vocation to reign over the world. The main idea is that Rome's destiny is evident in the sense of right and in the sense of common weal demonstrated by its assemblies and by its citizens. In this manner the strict submission and, if necessary, the sacrifice of private interest to the common good is perceived as the sign — clear, though not miraculous — of Rome's chosen status. Undoubtedly, at one point Dante goes so far as to grant the Romans a love of justice and peace, and to attribute to them, against all likelihood, concern for the salvation of the human race. But this idealized picture, and Dante's use of passages from Cicero, should not make us lose sight of his theologico-political argument: any one person's self-effacement in front of the City, or promptness to *die for one's country*, demonstrates the principle that the whole is more important than the part. In this regard, there is no need to call upon providence to understand this truth. As the conclusion to the passage in question states: 'there are some judgements of God which human reason can arrive at by its own unaided efforts' (II, vii, 2). Dante relies on Aristotle again, but he introduces a new element; the logic is embedded in the life of a people, whose members have, in a way, incorporated the need to abandon their particularity in favour of that which alone has full dignity: the community. It is therefore not enough to acknowledge, through the workings of the intellect, that neither thumb, hand, nor arm have their end in themselves, and that the same is true of family, village, city, and kingdom. It must be understood that Roman citizens have in a way interiorized nature's design, that they give themselves to the whole, and that in this way they prove to be potential citizens of the human race.

As commentators of the *Monarchia* point out, Dante's thinking was partly formed through contact with the teachings of the jurists of his day. Kantorowicz, in particular, notes that Dante's teacher, Remigio de' Girolami — himself a student of Thomas — was not satisfied with teaching that the whole is alone in actuality, while the part is in potentiality, and so citizens should love their country more than themselves. Remigio was not afraid to argue that if a man's city were destroyed that person would lose both his status as a citizen and his status as a man. Kantorowicz tells us that Remigio, that 'curious thomistic proto-Hegelian, was an extremist of anti-individualism'.[15] Yet the picture that Dante paints of the great Roman citizens stems from a different source of inspiration. It is in Livy that Dante finds the examples of individuals whose actions are to the glory of Rome, because they always bear the marks of devotion to the common good and of personal nobility. Livy's work had certainly been known to a small number of scholars for centuries, but Dante's use of it is no less striking because of that. Cincinnatus, Fabritius, Camillus, the first Brutus, the two Decii, and Cato are all figures in whom Roman virtue can be discerned — the virtue, that is, of an *active life* spent serving one's country and freedom. It is impossible, moreover, not to notice that Dante celebrates the heroes of the 'Republic'. Of course, he is following Livy. But, since

---

15   Kantorowicz, *The King's Two Bodies*, p. 479.

his aim is to prove the benefits of universal monarchy, it is surprising that he does not even mention Caesar, and that, instead, he describes Cato as 'the most stern guardian of liberty' (II, v, 15). Cato, whom Dante had already admired in the *Comedy*, had voluntarily killed himself on hearing of Caesar's victory. Note that this paradox was to attract the attention of the Florentine humanists who, at the end of the *Trecento*, asserted the excellence of the Republic and argued amongst themselves over how to interpret Dante's thought. Compared to the praise of Cato, the condemnation of Brutus, buried deep in Hell by the author of the *Comedy*, was able to be presented as of a purely symbolic order, with Caesar's murderer paling under the figure of the transgressor who attacked the universal monarchy. However strange this version of Brutus's conduct might seem, it is not, after all, implausible, since Dante himself calls for a distinction between the symbolic and literal meanings of the *Comedy*.

What is certain, if we stick to the *Monarchia*, is that its author wants to reproduce the genesis of the Empire and show that the seeds of the truth which occurred in the time of Augustus had been sown at Rome's beginnings and had been constantly growing throughout the course of its history, both in the organization of its institutions and in the actions of its players. This intention signals a break with Aristotle. Contradicting what had been suggested in Book I, the task of political philosophy is not to define good constitutions or weigh the merits of different systems of government, but rather to discover the progress of reason and right. This does not mean that observing the course of events is sufficient to appreciate this progress; the past only becomes clear for someone who knows the concepts of reason and right. However, this knowledge is itself not purely atemporal. Aristotelian knowledge remains unsurpassable, insofar as it is fundamental, but the work of the intellect and the explanation of the founding principles benefit from the experience of humanity.

THE TWO SOVEREIGNTIES

Does the authority of the Monarch derive directly from God or from another, a minister or vicar of God? Just as the principle of the answer to the question posed in the second Book could be found in the first Book, so the question raised in the third Book has already been resolved by the end of the second Book. But it is important for the question to be examined closely for its political significance and for how topical it remains. Dante, then, undertakes a refutation of the arguments of his adversaries. He bestows a singular philosophical breadth on this undertaking and, once more, discovers truths which no one had yet explored. The supporters of the thesis that he wants to overturn fall into three categories: firstly, the Supreme Pontiff and, in his wake, other shepherds of the Christian flock; secondly, those who, motivated by their cupidity, falsely proclaim their love for the Church and hate the very name of emperor; thirdly, the followers of a tradition which has been reduced to fidelity to the *Decretals*, as a result of a double ignorance of both theology and philosophy. Does it not seem as if Dante, like one of his Roman heroes, Horace, separates and isolates his adversaries so that he is able to defeat them by three successive trials by combat? To tell the truth, the second category hardly interests him at all. As for the decretalists, he counters that their sources are late and cannot have the same value as either the Old and the New Testaments, which preceded the establishment of the Church, or the synods, which accompanied its early development. His true adversaries are the defenders (said to be in good faith) of the Church and of pontifical authority. These he will hunt down in every way possible.

For example, he objects that it is not true that the sun and moon represent spiritual and temporal power, since the Book of Genesis teaches that both were created on the fourth day and man on the sixth, and if God's creature had remained in his perfect state, government would have been unnecessary. It is, equally, not true that the fact that Moses conferred spiritual power upon Levi before Judas received temporal power can be used as an argument in favour of the latter being subject to the former, for this would mean confusing the question of birth with that of authority. Nor is it true that Christ's double sovereignty can justify that of the Pope, since the Son of God never wanted to wield temporal power and, moreover, a vicar only ever represents his lord, whoever he may be, and is never equal to him. Nor is it even true that the image of the two swords signifies the two forms of power, for this doctrine relies on a false interpretation of Scripture. Nor, finally, is it true that Constantine could have given the seat of the Empire to Pope Sylvester, since, his duty commanding him to maintain humanity in common obedience, it was not at all in his power to divest himself of that responsibility; meanwhile, for its part, the Church could not have received anything, insofar as it had been forbidden from possessing temporal goods. Throughout all these arguments great pains are taken to make evident to its full extent the necessary distinction between the office and its custodian: the latter, as an individual, having no right to contradict the authority invested in him.

But let us leave the list of objections there in order to highlight two passages in which the philosophical stakes of the quarrel are revealed. Dante had suggested that the defenders in good faith of the Church were as ignorant in philosophy as they were in theology. He thus ends up dismantling an argument which is supposedly founded on Aristotelian principles (III, xii, 1): since all things belonging to the same species must be referred to one thing alone, which is the measure of the rest, so the human race must be referred to one man alone and, since this man could only be either Pope or Emperor, it must be concluded that he be Pope, for no one can argue that there is anybody above the Pope. In point of fact, let us explain in order to clarify this statement that Frederick II for his part never dreamt of subjecting the Pope to his authority. In order to prove the flawed nature of this logic, Dante introduces a new distinction between that which comes under the category of a *substance* and that which comes under the category of a *relationship*. The substance of man, which characterizes his species, is one thing; quite another is the relation established within the species, which characterizes such and such a mode of authority. Both Pope and Emperor are thus reducible in one sense to the man who is perfectly man, or, in Dante's terms, to the *optimus homo*, the perfect man. In a second sense, however, they are defined according to the relationship which is enshrined in their respective offices — a relationship which appertains to *paternitas* for the one and, for the other, to *dominatio* (a term which includes both the idea of absolute power and the idea of the exercise of government). Thus they are according to one measure reducible, and by another irreducible, the one to the other.

Any reader tempted to think that this argument is yet another dictated purely by the requirements of the polemic would soon be proven wrong. In effect, returning to the first question, as if that had not already been answered,

Dante claims that he has only demonstrated that the Emperor's authority does not depend on that of the Pope, but that he has yet to prove categorically that the Emperor's authority derives directly from God. This seems to me to be a simple pretext for going beyond the limits of his explicit aim. Effectively, he establishes that humans have a corruptible and an incorruptible nature, and that, necessarily feeling the effects of these two natures, humans are thus the only beings to be destined for two ultimate goals: on the one hand, happiness in this life, which consists in the exercise of one's own virtues, both intellectual and moral, the image of which is given to us by the earthly paradise; on the other hand, the happiness of eternal life to which humans can raise themselves only thanks to divine illumination, through the theological virtues, the image of which is given to us by the heavenly paradise (III, xvi, 3–7). At this point, Dante declares that he has finished his task and has fully answered the three questions set. Let us say that he has won the combat, or rather the series of trials by combat which he had undertaken.

Notwithstanding, the interpretation of Book III runs into striking difficulties. It is already surprising that the distinction between corruptible and incorruptible human nature, linked as it is to the distinction between body and soul, requires the distinction between two ultimate goals: happiness on earth, where the human condition is that of a mortal being, and eternal happiness. In passing, Dante invokes Aristotle, who teaches in the second book of *On the Soul* "'And it [the soul] alone, being immortal, can be separated from the corruptible'" (III, xvi, 4–5). Thus he does not hide the fact that philosophy already points, without the help of theology, to the idea of an ultimate goal which is not temporal. Why then does he deem it useful to specify, a few lines further on, that respect for the teachings of philosophy and the practice of moral and intellectual virtues are only the means of achieving the first goal of humanity, that which humanity pursues in its capacity as corruptible beings? Étienne Gilson does not linger on this question, but he leads us back to it when he endeavours to grasp the new interpretation of Christianity given by Dante. Gilson notes that the author of the *Monarchia* remains entirely in agreement with Saint Thomas in defining the relationship between priesthood and Empire; he neither isolates the two from each other, nor subordinates one to the other. The first proposition goes without saying; the second is supported by two references in the text. In effect Dante writes:

> as far as functioning better and more efficaciously is concerned, [the moon] receives something from the sun, namely abundant light; having received this, it operates more efficaciously. Thus I say that the temporal realm does not owe its existence to the spiritual realm, nor its power (which is its authority), and not even its function in an absolute sense; but it does receive from it the capacity to operate more efficaciously through the light of grace which in heaven and on earth the blessing of the supreme Pontiff infuses into it. (III, iv, 19–20)

Moreover, Dante grants at the end of the third Book that the prince owes some submission to the Supreme Pontiff 'since this earthly happiness is in some sense ordered towards immortal happiness' (III, xvi, 17–18). He concludes: 'Let Caesar therefore show that reverence towards Peter which a firstborn son should show his father, so that, illumined by the light of paternal grace, he may the more effectively light up the world' (III, xvi, 18). Gilson thus considers that 'the influence exerted by the Pope over the

Emperor is analogous to that of a blessing, i.e. of a form of grace.'[16] Is this simply a concession? The commentator rejects this suspicion: 'By reducing the problem of the two powers to a particular case of the general problem of nature and grace Dante was, incontestably, locating it in its true sphere.'[17] Thomas remains the authority, since, in his eyes, 'the peculiar effect of grace is not to vindicate nature or to suppress it, but to perfect it.'[18] In contrast, Dante is deemed to differentiate himself from Thomas through his wish to eliminate the principle of subordination, which governs the relationships between the different spheres, in order to replace that principle with the principle simply of co-ordination between the different authorities. For all that, the conclusion ought not to imply an opposition between a Christian and a pagan world, but rather 'two different dispositions of the Christian world'.[19]

This thesis is perhaps to be linked to the desire to tone down Dante's very evident dualism. Without erasing this dualism, Gilson reduces its impact by attributing to Dante the idea of a tripartite authority within which each element would come under a different category. To the Pope and the Emperor, who, as we have seen, are each put into a different category of relationship, Gilson adds the *optimus homo*, in which they each find, to a certain extent, their measure. Thus we are presented with a picture which includes: in the uppermost part, God; in the middle part, laid out symmetrically, the category of substance, the category of the relationship of paternity, and the category of the relationship of government; then, in the lowest part, the

---

16   Gilson, *Dante the Philosopher*, p. 187.
17   Ibid.
18   Ibid.
19   Ibid., p. 188.

related figures of the Pope, the Emperor, and the perfect man.[20] Finally, having examined the signs of dualism in Dante, Gilson returns to the theme of a no less fundamental trinity:

> Nothing could be clearer than the distinction between these three authorities: philosophy, which teaches us the *whole* truth about the natural goal of man; theology, which alone leads us to our supernatural goal; finally, political power, which, holding human greed in check, constrains men, by the force of the law, to respect the natural truth of the philosophers and the supernatural truth of the theologians.[21]

Now, besides the fact that Dante never at any point presents the perfect man as an authority, the distinction established between that which pertains to substance and that which pertains to relationship prevents him from so doing: authority can only be understood as relationship. Kantorowicz, who re-establishes the importance of this distinction, argues against Gilson that Dante is radically dualistic. Rightly struck by the extraordinary audacity with which Dante devises the idea of happiness in this life and of an earthly paradise, and likewise the idea that individuals come into possession of their *humanitas* by the exercise of intellectual and moral virtues alone, Kantorowicz sees in Dante's *Monarchia* an attempt to 'build up a whole sector of the world which was independent not only of the pope, but also of the Church and, virtually, even of the Christian religion'.[22]

---

20   Ibid., p. 190.
21   Ibid., p. 196.
22   Kantorowicz, *The King's Two Bodies*, p. 457.

It is true that in certain respects this enterprise was not new. Dante joins forces, against the group of hierocrats, known as monists, with the moderate supporters of the division of temporal and spiritual power, known as dualists, of whom the most eminent in the twelfth century was Huguccio of Pisa. But Dante goes much further than them in neglecting the position of the Emperor as a member of the Church and his submission in religious matters.[23] According to Kantorowicz, whose interpretation seems to me to be wholly convincing, Dante conceives for the first time of two worlds which are not only distinct but in a way autonomous — *humanitas* and *christianitas* — that is to say, two models, one centred on the human and the other on theology. However, the critic here discovers two versions of the mystical body, that of the Church and that of Humanity. Thus he substitutes a different picture to that of Gilson: one in which the Pope and the Emperor are linked symmetrically to God, because of their authority, and to Man because of their substance.[24] Consequently, the Emperor bears the marks of the perfect man; the idea of man, as understood by philosophy, is imprinted in him. Indeed, what would become of the Emperor if he were not to spread, by his own work, by his human virtues, philosophical truth?

It is therefore pointless to get caught up in choosing between a Christian and a pagan Dante. His mystical belief in the One bears the sign of Christian thought, without him conceding anything to dogma in his conception of human autonomy. Kantorowicz pushes this interpretation as far as possible by suggesting that the progression of the human race towards its perfection coincides with the

---

23   Ibid., p. 456.
24   Ibid., p. 461 n. 31.

restoration of the state in which the first man lived, or, to be more precise, with the reconstitution of the body of Adam before the Fall. But it is true that, however ingenious this argument may be, it must again be admitted that nothing in the text justifies it, and that it is difficult to see why, if such was his thinking, Dante would have failed to say as much. Moreover, how are we to imagine that the moral and intellectual virtues would suffice to reach the creature who had still not touched the tree of knowledge? And does not this supposition also have the problem of conferring a final theological meaning on the Monarchy?

Perhaps we need to be careful not to want to reduce all of Dante's arguments to one common denominator. He does not suggest that anyone can occupy the place from which truth would ceaselessly flow. Certainly, notions of happiness, paradise, the excellence of man, and the perfect state of the human race all point to the Absolute. But I am still not certain that we have understood them correctly. Dante sows doubt when he warns that the literal meaning can be accompanied by an allegorical meaning, a moral meaning, and an anagogical meaning (a higher or spiritual meaning). This understanding of meaning as fourfold remains faithful to the teaching of theologians. However, it is helpful to see how Dante uses it and how he illustrates it in the Letter which he addresses to Can Grande dedicating *Paradiso* to him. Taking the example of one psalm (113, v. 1), he proposes the following commentary:

> if we consider the letter alone, the thing signified
> to us is the going out of the children of Israel from
> Egypt in the time of Moses; if the allegory, our
> redemption through Christ is signified; if the moral
> sense, the conversion of the soul from the sorrow
> and misery of sin to a state of grace is signified; if the
> anagogical, the passing of the sanctified soul from

the bondage of the corruption of this world to the liberty of everlasting glory is signified.[25]

He adds that these last two senses 'may [...] in a general sense be termed allegorical, inasmuch as they are different (*diversi*) from the literal or historical'.[26] Clearly, here the interpretation is applied to the Scripture. But Dante moves away from theology when he invites us to read his poetic oeuvre in the same way as the Bible. In the same letter, he states that his aim was 'to remove those living in this life from a state of misery, and to bring them to a state of happiness'.[27] He offers the following explanation:

> The subject, then, of the whole work, taken in the literal sense only, is the state of souls after death, pure and simple. For on and about that the argument of the whole work turns. If, however, the work be regarded from the allegorical point of view, the subject is man according as by his merits or demerits in the exercise of his free will he is deserving of reward or punishment by justice.[28]

Henri de Lubac points out that Boccaccio reiterates the same attempt at interpretation in his *Life of Dante*. He also goes on to quote Coluccio Salutati (the famous humanist, chancellor of Florence in the last decades of the *Trecento*), a great admirer of Dante, who asks his interlocutor:

---

25   'Epistola X: To Can Grande della Scala', in Dante Alighieri, *Epistolae: The Letters of Dante*, ed. and trans. by Paget Toynbee (Oxford: Clarendon, 1920), pp. 160–211 (p. 199). [Translator's note: Lefort cites the Letter to Can Grande from the passages included in Lubac, *Exégèse médiévale*, II.2, pp. 322–23.]

26   Ibid., p. 199.

27   Ibid., p. 202.

28   Ibid., p. 200.

> Do you not see that sacred literature, the whole
> body of Holy Scripture, is, rightly considered, noth-
> ing else in its method of expression than poetry?
> For, when we are speaking of God or of incorporeal
> beings nothing is literally true, but beneath that sur-
> face of fiction there is nothing that is not true. And
> what other objection can you have to poetry? What
> is there about it that you can find to condemn? If
> you object to its method of expression you are be-
> yond a doubt condemning sacred literature and the
> Holy Scriptures.[29]

Of course, the *Monarchia* belongs to a different genre than
poetry, but it would be wrong to want to stick simply to its
literal meaning. Instead, it would be worth examining its
allegorical meaning and, in so doing, we should no longer
worry about the difficulty of reconciling philosophy and
theology.

Ought we not to examine the theme of justice (which
Gilson himself observes is present throughout) and the
significance of the dichotomy between paternity deprived
of power and a government to whom everyone is subjected? Ought we not also to wonder about the allegorical
meaning of happiness in this life? Dante tells us that we
can reach the latter through philosophical teachings on
condition that we follow these in our works, in accordance
with the moral and intellectual virtues (III, xvi, 8). This
last clarification deserves our attention. The importance of
Aristotle does not make us forget the importance of Virgil,
or of Cicero, nor even the importance of Cato. Similarly,
the full dignity of the human race does not mean that its

---

29 Coluccio Salutati, 'Letters in Defence of Liberal Studies', in Ephraim
Emerton, *Humanism and Tyranny: Studies in the Italian Trecento* (Cambridge, MA: Harvard University Press, 1925), pp. 285–377 (p. 316).
[Translator's note: Lefort cites this passage in French from Lubac, *Exégèse médiévale*, II.2, p. 324.]

final state can be easily defined; perhaps we are to understand that humanity has the power to wrest itself from its divisions and recognize itself as the same in the variety of its expressions. Notwithstanding, Dante does not suggest the image of a world dozing in peace and venerating its master, but rather that of a universal political society, fully awake, in which everyone understands their duty. At one point Gilson writes that 'Humanity first presented itself to the European consciousness merely as a secularized imitation of the religious notion of a Church.'[30] However, the term 'secularization' lends itself to too many uses.[31] In this case, it hides a fundamental difference between the principle of free will and the principle of faith. Kantorowicz understands the novelty of Dante more clearly when he highlights that opposition to the papacy and to the Church contains at least potentially a break with the Christian conception of the human condition. Must we not in effect agree that the notion of the earthly paradise has not only an allegorical meaning, but also a polemical import? There is something provocative in Dante's language which cannot have escaped his contemporaries.

DANTE AND CIVIC HUMANISM

On every page, the *Monarchia* bears the marks of medieval thought. Be that as it may, this observation should not lead us to neglect all that the text heralds. It is a major source of modern thought on which the Florentine humanists were the first to draw, followed by a number of writers who gained from this first shaking up of Christian political theology and ancient political philosophy the power

---

30   Gilson, *Dante the Philosopher*, p. 179.

31   [Translator's note: The French term here is 'laïcisation'.]

to seek in their turn a new start. Hans Baron — though we owe to him invaluable information about the influence exerted by Dante — estimates that it is only at the end of the *Trecento* that we find a new understanding of both history and political life being combined with the *studia humanitatis*. The flourishing of what Baron calls 'civic humanism' seems to him to be linked to the creation of a new group of intellectuals rooted in their city — a group who defended in the same breath the cause of the Republic and the ideal of a learned culture, and who condemned obscurantism as a product of both a period of darkness and of tyranny. Baron finds only one precedent for this movement: the spirit of freedom which reigned momentarily, around 1300, in Padua, Vicenza, Verona, and Milan, before being quashed when these communes were subjugated. Throughout most of the *Trecento*, according to Baron, humanists devoted themselves to purely literary research, going from court to court without any awareness of their citizenship.[32] For Baron, Dante would be one of these cosmopolitan intellectuals, obliged through exile to err across Italy, except that in his case he made himself a theorist of Empire. His ideas were soon to belong to a past age; his uprootedness would condemn him to profess an abstract form of humanism.

But why then, one wonders, does his influence remain so acute? Why is the homage paid to him addressed not only to the poet, to the writer who was the first to make the Tuscan tongue glorious? Why was Coluccio Salutati, the precursor of new ideas, so interested in him? Was it because Salutati's republican convictions were not yet wholly fixed, as would seem to be suggested by the *De Tyranno*, written

---

32   Hans Baron, *The Crisis of the Early Italian Renaissance*, 2nd, rev. edn (Princeton, NJ: Princeton University Press, 1966), p. 5.

at the end of his life and in which the power *of one alone* is justified by circumstances? But why does Leonardo Bruni decide to write in his turn a *Life of Dante* — that same Bruni in whom Baron recognizes the purest representative of civic humanism, he who never ceased praising the Republic, who defined both the correctly balanced system of government and the armed citizen, with long-lasting effects? Why is he so concerned to purge Dante of the suspicion of having condemned Brutus? And why does this same concern recur in the works of humanists in the following two centuries? Why, finally, is the trace of Dante still perceptible in Machiavelli's *Discourses* (at least in the first Book)? It is true that the latter overturns Dante's theories, considers the disagreements that Rome experienced to be beneficial, and judges the government of several to be superior to the government of one alone. Yet the fact remains that Machiavelli's allusions to Dante's opinion must have been important to his readers.

Whether he inspired praise or refutation, Dante was never forgotten. And forgotten he could not be, for his work contained something other than a theory of Empire. He had opened a new field to thought, given form to humanity, broken the image of cyclical time, bestowed upon life on earth its dignity, and fully rehabilitated the part therein of the *vita activa*, without ceasing to hold the highest opinion of the *vita contemplativa*. Finally, he had conjured up an idea of the oeuvre — of the work of thought governed by the demands of beginnings and unveiling — which was to be essential for all subsequent philosophical writers. To cite only his great detractor, is it not clear that Machiavelli paraphrases to a great extent the prologue of the *Monarchia* in the preface to his *Discourses*?

> Although owing to the envy inherent in man's nature it has always been no less dangerous to discover new ways and methods than to set off in search of new seas and unknown lands [...], none the less, impelled by the natural desire I have always had to labour, regardless of anything, on that which I believe to be for the common benefit of all, I have decided to enter upon a new way, as yet untrodden by anyone else.[33]

The image of exploration is different, and God is passed over in silence. However, there is still the same claim of discovery and innovation, the same expression of a desire to serve the common good, and the same insistence on the riskiness of the undertaking.

THE WORK OF THE OEUVRE

We have many reasons to return to Dante's oeuvre.[34] Not only did it fuel the thinking of Italian humanists from Petrarch to Machiavelli, but it also spurred the imagination of princes across modern Europe and equally led to reflection on the myth of the One. In the sixteenth century, it was highly attractive to great monarchs, as well as to jurists, theologians, and poets who celebrated their power. It seems paradoxical that it was at a point when kingdoms had proved to be the only powers which counted, when the

---

33 Niccolò Machiavelli, *The Discourses*, ed. by Bernard Crick, trans. by Leslie J. Walker, rev. by Brian Richardson (London: Penguin, 2013), p. 97.

34 [Translator's note: The section heading translates the French 'le travail de l'œuvre', which repeats parts of the title of Lefort's doctoral thesis on Machiavelli, *Le Travail de l'œuvre Machiavel* (Paris: Gallimard, 1972), partially translated into English as *Machiavelli in the Making*, trans. by Michael B. Smith (Evanston, IL: Northwestern University Press, 2012). For Lefort's explanation of this methodological formula, consult the first part of his treatise: 'The Question of the Oeuvre', pp. 3–59.]

notion of borders had become decisive, and when the new masters had successfully emancipated themselves from the oversight of the papacy — some without relinquishing established religion, others by supporting the Reformation — that the idea of a world united under one temporal and spiritual authority was resurrected and that, at the same time, Dante's theories were revived. Now, let us not forget that it was during this period, in the middle of the century, that there appeared the work which contains probably the most radical criticism of the power of one alone: La Boétie's *Discourse on Voluntary Servitude*. There are many indications that the author's target in this text was, beyond the contemporary theory of monarchy, Dante's treatise. What chord had been struck in people's hearts by this thinker whom some considered as the last spokesperson of medieval beliefs, so that, more than two hundred years after he wrote his work, his ideas should thus continue to resonate? The effectiveness of the representation of a *dominus mundi*, of an emperor heir of Caesar Augustus, is troubling in Europe at a time when the characteristics of the nation state are being fully drawn. Moreover, the myth of the empire will gain new life subsequently in different forms. Suffice it to mention the ambitions of France under Napoleon, of Austria or Germany during the nineteenth century, or even the large-scale colonial projects which preserve some traces of this myth. Universalist aspirations and the desire for unlimited expansion are two sides of the same coin.

It also seems paradoxical that the traces of Dante's ideas are still visible in periods when sovereignty has been detached from the monarch. These traces are discernible in the theologico-political debates which accompany the

English Revolution,[35] and then the birth of new republics in America. Moreover, however new the principles to which the French Revolution claims to adhere, it is notable that its most famous interpreter, Michelet, offers us some of the most telling evidence of Dante's influence. Naturally, these last few references might cause some surprise. What would remain — one might well ask — of the fabric of the treatise, once its principal part, the monarch, has been amputated? But I have insisted on the fact that the figure of the sovereign of the world, as conceived by Dante, is inserted into a composition all of whose elements are destined to demonstrate the resplendent virtue of the One. The idea of the omnipotence of the monarch proves, in effect, to be closely connected to ideas of justice, peace, and concord, but also to the idea of a *renovatio* — of a return to the perfect moment when the fullness of time manifested itself —, to the idea of the legacy of a chosen people, of whom the double image is provided by the Jewish and the Roman peoples (is it not written in *Convivio* IV, v, 6 that the birth of David coincided with that of Aeneas?), and, finally, to the idea of a sharing between the destiny of an individual in search of the salvation of their soul and the destiny of the human race in search of its unity. Does the recurrence of these themes, each of which will be reworked in different circumstances in different countries, not bear witness to their affinities and to the formation of one of the templates of modern politics?

It is true that Dante's reader seeks first of all to assess the break that Dante effectuates with important Christian authors, particularly with the Thomism which had tried to incorporate Aristotle's principles. Thus the reader discovers the work which enabled Dante to take advantage of

---

35   [Translator's note: i.e. the English Civil War.]

both the speculation and the narratives of his predecessors in order to make a new oeuvre. At the same time, the reader notices Dante's receptiveness to the thought of others and to the events both of the past and of his time, his ability to allow himself to be *worked* by everything which came to his attention. However, it is not only looking back in time, to the conception of the oeuvre, and seeking to reconstitute its genesis, which grants access to this oeuvre. Whether or not the reader realizes it, they are guided by the signs of its fecundity; they are alerted by the impact that it has had in the course of a history unimaginable for its author. This impact highlights particular arguments of whose importance the author was unaware. For example, Bruni or Machiavelli's reading encourages us to understand the role that Dante gave to the citizens of the Roman republic in the formation of humanity. Or, equally, considering the use that both princes and political thinkers have, at different points in time, been able to make of his ideas leads Dante's reader to examine the symbol of the One. In short, the oeuvre continues to reveal itself through the work of time, in the sense that it shows itself able to summon up beliefs or thoughts connected to a new experience of the world and in the sense that history renders visible everything which was implicitly brought into play when the text shook up the traditions and inaugurated a new theologico-political language. If, then, the birth of the oeuvre bears the mark of time, so too does its fate, although in a different fashion. The need to understand what Dante meant remains, but it does not entail disregarding what he announced, since, all things considered, it is the questions he raised which matter to us. And these questions are all the more pressing when we find them in transpositions, or even in distortions of his theory, or better still on examining the criticisms which he inspired in thinkers who established a close relationship with him. Let us recall what Dante says in the *Convivio*: 'And all our troubles, if we really search out their origins, derive in some way from not knowing how to use time' (IV, ii, 10).

THE IDEA OF UNIVERSAL MONARCHY IN THE SIXTEENTH CENTURY

The essays which Frances Yates has brought together in *Astraea* and which are dedicated to the rebirth of the myth of the Empire in the sixteenth century help us to understand what is meant by 'how to use time.'[36] This historian demonstrates that Dante's treatise sheds light on the symbolism of the Empire. She does not hide the distance which separates Dante from the propagandists of Charles V, Elizabeth I, or the kings of France (from Francis I to Henry IV). She gives many examples of the influence that Dante exerted. But it is sufficient to note the reappearance of the imperial idea — of a constellation of symbols which were found for the first time in his oeuvre — to be persuaded that he was not a dreamer. Rather, he knew how to discover if not, as he claimed, previously unknown truths, at least signs of the new legitimacy of political power in Europe. After all, let us not forget that at that time Philip the Fair was already rebelling against the pope and claiming to be a very Christian king in order to affirm the sovereignty of the State and that, here and there, the phrase *rex imperator in suo regno* was being established. From Yates's enquiry it turns out that the ideas which Dante had brought together granted consistency to what we might call a historical imaginary.

36　Frances A. Yates, *Astraea: The Imperial Theme in the Sixteenth Century* (London: Routledge & Kegan Paul, 1975).

Moreover, those who exploited this set of images, capitalizing on the events in their own day, notably Charles V and then Elizabeth I, acted as relays in its dissemination, all the while obscuring its origin.

The example of Charles V is revealing. We are reminded that, as a result of a lucky combination of circumstances, his inheritance included on the one hand Spain, which had recently been unified owing to the union of Castile and Aragon, in addition to the Kingdom of Sicily, and on the other hand, a huge expanse of land consisting of the Duchy of Burgundy, the Netherlands, and Austria. This seems sufficient to understand his desire to raise himself above his powerful rivals. But his ambitions were different in scope. The image which he presents designates him as the emperor whose portrait Dante had drawn. He presents himself as an agent of God, tasked with a universal mission; he claims to reform the Church and destroy Christianity's enemies. Frances Yates brings out convincing signs of Dante's influence. The Italian Mercurio Gattinara, close adviser of the monarch and his old tutor, was a fervent admirer of the *Monarchia*; we know that he asked Erasmus — albeit unsuccessfully — to prepare a new edition of it. Meanwhile, Antonio Guevara, the king's historiographer and court preacher, invoked Dante's arguments in his book, the *Relox de principes*, 'which was widely read all over Europe'.[37] One of the references mentioned by Yates is particularly striking, because it demonstrates Charles V's influence in Europe. In his *Orlando furioso*, Ariosto has a prophetess announce the unification of the world under a universal monarch heir to Augustus, Trajan, and Severus. A sovereign stemming from the union of Austria and Aragon will bring back to earth Astraea–

---

37   Ibid., p. 22.

Justice, and all the exiled virtues.[38] The prophecy has to do with both the coming of a new emperor and the discovery of continents unknown to the Romans. Just as for Dante the expansion of the empire which led to the census of humanity coincided with the coming Christ, so too the discovery of America is the sign of a revelation. According to Yates, this theme reveals the meaning of Charles V's famous emblem, which included the two columns of Hercules accompanied by the motto *plus oultre*: the new empire is thus considered to extend beyond the limits of that of Rome. That this emblem should have fascinated the monarchs of England and France is a clear indication of the importance of what I have described as the relaying of the imperial myth. When she highlights that 'Charles's device was known throughout Europe' and 'raised again the phantom of empire', Yates sheds new light on the history of ideas.[39] In this history, it is not so much, as I have said, the references to Dante which matter, but rather the transformations of some of his ideas which occur taking the framework which he constructed as a starting-point. These transformations are only comprehensible if we explore in each case the circumstances in which they were able to arise and the intentions of the new political players.

The cult of Elizabeth I was partly based on the model of that of Charles V, although it reactivated the representations of a universal monarchy for new ends and in a different national context. Elizabeth benefited from the renaissance of arts and letters which was fuelled by the passion for ancient history. At the same time, the establishment of a strong military power and a politics of expansion were pursued under her rule. It is telling that her glory

---

38   Ibid., p. 53.
39   Ibid., p. 23.

reached its apogee, as Yates remarks, at the time of the victory over the Spanish Armada. This was a highly symbolic event, not only because it freed England from the threat hanging over it from its most fearful adversary, but also because it demonstrated its chosen status in the fight — Dante would have said, in the trial by combat — for world empire. The promise contained in this victory responded in a way to the promise that Spain saw in the discovery of America: mastery of the seas announced the end of the earth's divisions.

In a way, Elizabeth's prestige came, like that of Charles V, from the belief that she was born under the sign of union. She united the two Roses, one the symbol of the House of Lancaster, the other the symbol of the House of York, just as the Spanish monarch benefited from the union of Castile and Aragon. This union seemed to announce the bringing together of all peoples under her reign. However, the imperial symbolism is reworked in a particular fashion, since if Elizabeth claimed also to be invested with a sacred mission, she was able to take advantage of England's break with Catholicism in order to give credence to the myth of 'a golden age of pure imperial religion'.[40] From this power of incarnating the Reformation, she gains new credentials for realizing universal monarchy and assuming the vocation which Dante assigned to his sovereign unrivalled on earth. It must be noted that Dante was not a precursor of Protestantism; Gilson has already denounced this fiction. Still, the advantages that the English monarchy derives from the combination of political power and religion are evident. And it must be admitted that Dante's arguments lend themselves to the use to which the English monarchy was able to put them. The writings of Bishop

---

40   Ibid., p. 39.

Jewel, who was familiar with Dante's work, bear witness to this use. Jewel accuses the pope of being responsible for the divisions in Christian society and recalls that Roman emperors sat on the Church councils in the early days of Christianity. An even more striking witness is John Foxe's book *Acts and Monuments*, one of the most widely disseminated works in the kingdom, present in most churches, and which makes Elizabeth an heir of Constantine (who himself was born of an English mother, in England even). With Foxe, who cites in his book a whole passage from Dante's *Monarchia*, imperial renaissance and religious reformation are elided. Still, it must be remarked that the Queen's genealogy is doubled. In addition to the image of Constantine as ancestor, there is a further image of a Trojan ancestor, a relative of Aeneas the founder of Rome, who supposedly founded London under the name *Troynavant*, the new Troy. This legend was no less present than the first, and is exploited by most of the Elizabethan poets. Thus we see the Christian and Virgilian traditions being intertwined in order to justify the election of the emperor and the emperor's people.

However, we would not grasp one of the most potent reasons for Elizabeth's chosenness were we to neglect her transfiguration into Astraea, the divine Justice whose presence Dante, as a reader of Virgil, announced alongside the emperor. It seems that this transfiguration came about from the start of her reign and provided an inexhaustible motif in the literature of the period. Themes of the Queen's chastity and her birth under the zodiacal sign of the Virgin were merged with the subject of the reappearance of Astraea which marks the return of Saturn's reign, the golden age. Without wishing to summarize Yates's argument and unable to give a sense of the richness of her documentation and commentaries (notably those inspired by Spenser's *Fairy Queen* and Shakespeare's *Titus Andronicus*), I would merely like to point out that the two portraits of the emperor and of justice are overlain by the portrait of a unique being who is, in this sense, without precedent. Her power is not only the sign of Astraea's invisible presence; Elizabeth is herself Astraea, the incarnation of Astraea. Marvellous is the condensation of celestial justice and of the monarch devoted to ruling the universe into one single person. Or rather, we might also say, marvellous is the doubling of the sovereign, at once suffused with the whiteness which — in Dante's words — 'does not admit of a more and a less' (I, xi, 3) and endowed with the will to command all human beings. Elizabeth proves herself to be both justice and judge; she unites heavenly and earthly life. In the series of figures of the king's two bodies, so insightfully studied by Kantorowicz, she deserves a special place, since, for those who venerate her, if not for the jurists, her immortality is almost manifest in her natural body.

Although Yates's studies contain a wealth of information about the French monarchy in the sixteenth century, notably concerning the staging of 'royal entrances' in the service of the imperial cult, as well as the support that the Pléiade poets offered to this cult, the case is too well known to be worth pausing over. Doubtless, it offers an unusual version of the rebirth of the Empire, since the sovereign takes advantage of Charlemagne's lineage and the miraculous conversion of Clovis. But once more we see belief in the divine mission of the king, dubbed 'Most Christian' (*Rex Christianissimus*), being interwoven with both the legend of Trojan origins (Francus, son of Hector, playing the role of an English Brutus) and the legend of the legacy of Augustus. Born under Francis I, the restorer of the golden age, and developed under Charles IX, the myth of the ruler of the world flourishes under Henry IV. Incarnating the union of the kingdom and that of the two faiths which divide the peoples, this last gave rise throughout the whole of Europe to the hope of a return of Astraea (a theme which circulated widely), of universal peace, and of the full legitimacy of political authority.[41]

THE TWO IMAGES OF THE NEW POLITICAL BODY

How could the project of universal monarchy formulated by Dante take shape within the space of a kingdom? This phenomenon seems less strange, if we consider that the representation of the One becomes newly effective once it is supported by the representation of a political body — a body circumscribed in space yet at the same time a mystical body which, as such, knows no limits.

Let us recall Gilson's observation: Thomas Aquinas never mentions the authority of the emperor, and is only interested in the relationship between the spiritual power of the pope and the temporal power of kings. Doubtless, these last seem to him to enjoy relative independence in the exercise of their government, which stems from the imperatives of the maintenance of society. They remain, nonetheless, subordinate to the supreme authority of the Vicar of Christ. Are they then sovereigns? Without a doubt, in the sense that in the domain which they administer, all human beings, regardless of their rank, must obey their king so that justice and peace may reign. The greatest guarantee of concord is in the government of a monarch. From this perspective, Thomism seems to unite the defence of dogma with realism. The pope's recognized supremacy

---

41   Ibid., p. 210.

does not lead to the fantasy of a theocracy. The recognized autonomy of kings does not mean that they can free themselves from the supervision of the guardian of divine law, but rather bears witness to the irreducibility of the temporal and the spiritual; it seems, moreover, in keeping with the needs of the time. In fact, the power of a few great princes proves only liable to rescue people from the arbitrary domination of lords, and to procure for the Church mediators on whom she can rely and who act as obstacles to the emperor's ambitions.

Nonetheless, how is it possible to admit the subordination of one sovereignty to another? I will note in passing that the question is so important as to continue to be asked subsequently, however different its terms, up to our own day. Once possessing sovereignty means having nobody higher than oneself in this world, how is it possible to conceive of partial sovereignty? From one perspective, theocracy is an illusion, in the sense that the state of the world means that it has no chance of being realized and in the sense that it contradicts the distinction between the spiritual and the temporal. Yet the fact remains that belief in the pope's sovereignty includes the possibility of being carried away by the idea of single command of the universe. Conversely, the government of a monarch cannot claim to elude the supervision of the head of the universal Church, but the office which he fills, and which places him above all others in his realm and makes him seem a unique being both in his own eyes and in those of his subjects, includes the possibility of being carried away by the idea of absolute power. Ultimately, there are no criteria able to decide definitively between what is temporal and what spiritual.

While Saint Thomas does not mention the role of the emperor, Dante has hardly any interest in the role of kings. His indifference towards the rise to power of a new type of political player seems to testify to an inability to decipher the meaning of history which is already being proclaimed in his day. Should we not, however, consider that in spite of his error, or perhaps as a result of it, Dante nonetheless uncovers particular features of the genesis of modern monarchies? The ambiguity which clings to the notion of sovereignty in medieval theory is in effect at the heart of his reflections. He does not deny that there are two sovereignties, but he conceives of them in such a way that they belong to two different spheres and cannot encroach upon each other. Sovereignty is, on the one hand, purely religious and, on the other, purely political; it resides either in *paternitas* or in *dominatio*. In the political sphere, it is at once spiritual and temporal; spiritual, since the monarch is the representative of humanity — a humanity which is part of God's creation and has its own end, the actualization of the intellective power.

Yet the use of the terms *spiritual* and *religious* is liable to be misunderstood, since the political has a religious as well as a philosophical meaning. Universal *civilitas* is religious in the sense that Christianity is inscribed in social institutions (an idea which will re-emerge, despite their very different experience of history, with certain nineteenth-century thinkers). It is also philosophical since Reason is supposed to govern all human beings. Now, is not this new idea of the political a guiding force in the development of monarchies? In effect, the king only appeared initially as the *primus inter pares*, even if he seemed to possess supernatural qualities; he remained caught up in a network of personal relationships shaped by reciprocal obligations of protection and fidelity. His authority, in contrast, stops being relative when it no longer depends principally on the allegiance of lords, but instead becomes the guarantor of the union of a people situated in a defined space and of their permanence in time.

Examining the conditions of this transformation would be of little relevance to our argument. Only one phenomenon calls for our attention: the kingdom is constituted as a political body by assimilating the symbols of the Church. Its subjects, whatever their status, appear as the members of this body; the king, like the head of the Church, is removed from all the rest and gains the power to incarnate a community, all the while standing at its head. From Kantorowicz's meticulous analysis let us remember that the political body, although it is organized as a functional body, comes to be defined as a mystical body modelled on the mystical body of the Church. The formation of the State at the end of the Middle Ages has, then, a dual aspect: on the one hand, the assertion of power and law over a territory, the delimitation of a political society between defined borders, and the concentration of means of power in the hands of the prince; on the other hand, and in parallel, the conversion of this territory into a holy land, the transfiguration of the State into a spiritual entity, and the investing of an originally divine authority in the person of the king.

We would be unable to comprehend the extent of this phenomenon were we not to remark that since the kingdom is conceived as a mystical body and the king as representing the One, the perspective widens so that the universe is incorporated into the kingdom and the world is subjugated by the one who renders the name of the One resplendent. Doubtless, the desire to conquer and to extend the limits of the power that has been gained ever further is not unique to modern princes. Yet it does seem as if their ambition takes on a new character as a result of their identification with a political community. This observation calls for some commentary. On the one hand, the kingdom differs from the city in its range and in the diversity of the forms of organization that it entails, but it shares some of the characteristics of cities through its cohesiveness and the sentiments of all belonging to the same homeland that it inspires. On the other hand, it differs from empire because of both the strict delineation of its territory and the link that it establishes between the sovereign and the nation, but it shares with empire the notion of a secular history which includes the Church as an institution and whose principal concern remains the conquest of sovereignty over the earth. Finally, if the image of the kingdom as a mystical body, a body which aims to include everything within itself, becomes clearer by considering the model provided by the empire, it is also vital to note that the Church was itself influenced by the monarchy. It was in answer to the constitution of the kingdom that the Church built its domain and tried to root its power in the world. Its early experience of rivalry with the empire led it to create a clergy detached from secular hierarchies. However, the instruments which it gave to its sovereignty, and thanks to which it gained the cohesiveness of a functional body, placed it in competition with the new monarchies.

In light of these concomitant developments, Dante's work becomes newly significant. Doubtless, Dante was not aware of Henry VII's weakness. For Dante, that Henry VII bore the title of emperor sufficed to make him appear the heir of Caesar Augustus and the guide of the whole of humanity. Dante was equally blind to the fact that this purported master of the world had to rely on the ever fragile allegiance of princes and lords whose effective power was not dependent on his. He ignored, likewise, the fact that Henry's authority was not grounded in a political community, did not benefit from being identified with a people, and floated, in a way, above Europe and even above Italy which was the cradle of the empire. In contrast, Dante was aware of the origins and the evolution of the Church and understood that pontifical monarchy had been established through usurpation and ran into contradiction once it attempted to appropriate ultimate sovereignty.

He suggests, moreover, a new and fruitful interpretation of Revelation, according to which Revelation is not limited to the message of the presence of God in each individual, but rather offers to humanity the sign both of its unity and of the meaning of history, a history which is at once providential and secular. What is thereby brought to the fore is the universal mission accomplished in the past by a particular people — on the one hand, the Jewish people obeying God's commandments; on the other hand, the Roman people guided by Justice — and their power to lead humanity towards its ultimate end. Dante draws out this idea of a chosen people, connected to that of the progress of the human race towards its perfection, from knowledge of Scriptures and from the books of classical writers. Monarchs are likely to seize this idea in order to establish a connection, in their own time, between the sovereign, the chosen people, the holy land, and the nation's genealogy. Dante provides monarchs with a source of inspiration on which they can draw once they think they possess the means of fulfilling their ambition. Regardless of the influence of his work, at a minimum it sheds light on the attempts to restore the empire in the sixteenth century.

Consequently, it is not enough to note the transfiguration of the kingdom into a mystical body, the translation of the ideal of *christianitas* within its limits. We must also consider the relationship established between the notion of a territory on which the drama of the world is being played out and a new understanding of time which eludes the Church. This understanding means conceiving of the secular history of a people, which leads back to a foundation as noble as Rome, and whose events announce world domination. Although the myth of empire is fuelled by legends which glorify the prince, they give a depth and meaning to time which had previously been hidden by theologians intent on parsimoniously taking from Antiquity only what agreed with their teaching. These legends afford the monarch credentials and a sacred function in addition to those of his divine office and remove him from the jurisdiction of the pope. At the same time, the nation benefits from being doubly chosen, since it owes its chosen status both to God's protection and to the succession of princes and generations which make up its history. The legend, incidentally, is greatly fuelled by newly gained knowledge of Antiquity; it is marked by humanist culture, its credibility enhanced by theorists, poets, and learned artists.

A sign that the cult of monarchy in the sixteenth century embodies a new conception of the political can be found in the persistence of representations associated with the figure of Elizabeth in England into the seventeenth century. I have already alluded to this phenomenon. In order to explore it, it would be necessary to follow the development of the belief in the exceptional destiny of the English people, whose origins, customs, and constant aspirations seem to demonstrate both that they are God's creation and that it was through their own power that they earned the right to mastery of the universe. I will note only that during the political and religious conflicts which had perturbed England since Mary's reign (under which there was a return to Catholicism) up until the period following the Revolution, the same argument is used in different forms. The nation's history and the signs of its chosen status make submission to an institution which claims to be invested in divine authority difficult. Those who put forward this argument first of all find that it is subsequently turned against them. Henry VIII's proclamation of an empire freed from any obedience to the Pope had already benefited from a widely shared belief in their nation's sovereignty since time immemorial. Such a conviction persisted amongst radical puritans who fled their country under Mary so as to protect their faith. They asserted that the individual was alone before God, and found in coming together and through shared discipline the energy to fight against evil in the world. Nor did they give up on the idea of England's sacred mission. These Marian exiles undertook, from Geneva, an active programme of propaganda against the Church and the government of the kingdom; they made themselves agents of God's law, rejected the legitimacy supposedly conferred on the institutions in place as a result of their ancient origins, and went so far as to demand a reform of the Reformation itself. Such was the strength of their criticism of the social order and their desire for change that one historian, Michael Walzer, considers them to be the first group of revolutionary intellectuals in Europe.[42]

Nonetheless, as J. G. A. Pocock has convincingly demonstrated, they never stopped considering themselves as both saints and English,[43] linking their chosen status

---

42 Michael Walzer, *The Revolution of the Saints: A Study in the Origins of Radical Politics* (Cambridge, MA: Harvard University Press, 1982).

43 J. G. A. Pocock, *The Machiavellian Moment: Florentine Political Thought and the Atlantic Republican Tradition* (Princeton, NJ: Princeton University Press, 1975).

to the existence of a people chosen by God. Pocock highlights this ambiguity and points out, besides, that their apocalyptic vision — which was without precedent in the other Protestant countries — was connected to their certainty that the time had come for England to take charge of the salvation of humanity and assume its destined role in the drama of sacred history. In addition, the saints' beliefs were to contribute to the defence of temporal power: the Pope appears as an impostor, because he promotes the belief that Christ remains present in the sacrament and in the institution of the Church; in contrast, the secular authority of the monarch has the merit of preserving the expectation of Christ's reign. In a striking turn of phrase that Dante would not, perhaps, have contradicted, Pocock notes that for the saints 'The *saeculum* was more truly Christian than the false pretense of eternity maintained by Rome.'[44]

In this new expression of the critique of religious institutions, the target was the Church of England in the early decades of the seventeenth century, accused of having arrogated for itself the prerogatives formerly exercised by the Roman Catholic Church. In the eyes of a number of puritans, who were loyal to the teachings of John Foxe, Laud's episcopacy committed the sin, not of contributing to the rise of absolutism, but of having contravened the principles on which the monarchy was founded. However, even more significant was the hostility which the saints themselves encountered. In their turn, they awakened the suspicion of wanting to suppress the chosen status from which, it was thought, the Commonwealth alone benefited. Many movements in the 1650s shared the view not only that no church, but also that no putative 'army of God' had the

---

44   Pocock, *The Machiavellian Moment*, p. 343.

right to govern public life or encroach upon the domain which came under the jurisdiction of the nation's sovereign powers. Such was the view of the Independents, which also emerges in the writings of Milton and Harrington. The definition, put forward by these two writers, of the citizen as God's Englishman is remarkable. So, too, is their fear of seeing, under the pretext of waiting for Christ, the efforts of the people to create for themselves free institutions be discredited — and, as a consequence, so also is their concern for the recognition (here I am paraphrasing Pocock) of the fact that the *saeculum*, and more precisely the restoration of a just constitution, is more authentically Christian than the dream of Christ's reappearance.

Harrington's famous book, *Oceana*, which is a landmark in the history of ideas, given the extent of its influence on eighteenth-century thinkers, reveals most clearly the intersections between the representations which emerged during the imperial renaissance and a new conception of the political. *Oceana* — which cannot be reduced to a utopia, since its references to the history of England are very evident — proposes to justify the accession of a new republic through an analysis of the combined evolution of property relations and power relations within the kingdom since the Norman invasion. However, the work connects the greatness of the Commonwealth to the virtue of its citizens who, like the Romans, enjoy freedom and constitute an armed people. At the same time, Harrington recognizes in this Commonwealth a new chosen nation, a new Israel. He deems it destined, like an empire, to unlimited expansion; finally, he goes so far as to ascribe to it immortality. There is no allusion to Dante, and no sign of his influence, and yet must it not be admitted that Elizabeth's reign, after the reign of Charles V, acted in turn to relay the ideas of the *Monarchia*? The monarch's sovereignty has migrated to the Commonwealth and the theory of the imperial republic has come to provide a new version of the universal city. Now this version in turn proves to be rich in subsequent developments. In 1776, the Americans will transform their resistance to the English parliament into revolution, and will fervently embrace republicanism by mobilizing all the motifs that we have thus far encountered: motifs of a chosen people, of a dual inheritance of the ancient city and of Israel, of a unique moment in which the history of humanity is revealed, even the motif of a society which is destined, for the first time, for immortality.

Doubtless, quite different are the principles which guided those involved in the French Revolution. The hatred inspired by the Church, as a result of its connections to political institutions, the destabilizing, even, of Christianity, over which the Catholic clergy had managed to preserve their monopoly, were not conducive to the development of a theory which would put France under the sign of having been doubly chosen. The dominant representation of France seems to have been that of a nation which brings enlightenment to the world, within which the Revolution marks the advent of a social order consonant with reason and the restitution to humanity of its natural right. However, this representation is far from accounting for the beliefs mobilized by the break with the monarchy of the Ancien Régime, as is proved by the debate instituted in the nineteenth century surrounding the relationship between the Revolution and Christianity. Here I will pause on the example of Michelet.

DANTE AND MICHELET

'How was the task of unfettering humankind accomplished in Europe?' asks Michelet in his *Introduction to World History* (written in the wake of the July Revolution).[45] His answer is that France is the great author of this work, whatever the merits of other nations. In order to justify France's eminence, he makes use of two images whose importance I have already noted: that of a nation's organic unity and that of the nation as a moral person. In France, he argues, 'The sign and warrant of a living organism [...] is present here in the highest degree.'[46] But soon afterwards he adds that France has achieved an 'intimate fusion of races' and that this constitutes 'the very identity of our nation, its personality'.[47] Moreover, Michelet more than once compares the mission that France is henceforth assuming with that which Rome had in Antiquity. The conclusion to his work asserts that 'Rome was the crux of the immense drama whose peripeteia France directs'.[48] In order to characterize Rome, he uses, incidentally, similar metaphors to those that France inspired: 'Rome is not an exclusive world'; 'She breathes in [...] the Latin [...] peoples', then, when they have become Roman, 'she breathes them out into her colonies.'[49] He explains: 'In this fashion she assimilated the whole world.'[50] In another passage, we learn

45 Jules Michelet, 'Introduction to World History (1831)', trans. by Flora Kimmich, in Michelet, *On History: Introduction to World History (1831); Opening Address at the Faculty of Letters, 9 January 1834; Preface to the History of France (1869)*, trans. by Flora Kimmich, Lionel Gossman, and Edward K. Kaplan (Cambridge: Open Book Publishers, 2013), pp. 23–118 (p. 37).

46 Ibid., p. 49.

47 Ibid., p. 50.

48 Ibid., p. 63.

49 Ibid., p. 32.

50 Ibid.

that 'This magnificent adoption of the peoples long led the Romans to believe that they had accomplished the great work of humanity'.[51] The belief that is imputed to them is the belief held by Dante. Michelet contradicts it, for, as he shows, Rome encountered 'the barbarians, the Christians, the slaves [who] were protesting, each in their own way, that Rome was not the city of the world, and in different ways they pulled that factitious unity apart'.[52]

But do we not recognize Dante's inspiration when — calling out in his habitual manner to the people who have rallied to Christianity and have eyes only for heaven — he exclaims: 'There you are now, divided into kingdoms, into monarchies, speaking twenty different tongues. What about the universal and divine city of which Christian charity gave you a presentiment and which you promised to realize here on earth?'[53] Like Dante, Michelet makes a distinction between the fate of individuals each attached to the salvation of their own souls and the fate of humanity in search of its identity. Thus he writes: 'the relation between God and man was simple then. The relation of humanity to itself in a divine society, that translation of heaven to earth, is a complex problem whose long solution may last the lifetime of the world.'[54] I have not forgotten that for Dante the solution had been discovered and that all that was necessary was for the peoples to make it work, whereas for Michelet, 'its beauty is in its unfolding, its infinite unfolding.'[55] Yet the fact remains that Michelet invokes a revelation made to humanity as a whole. He puts forward this idea at several points. According to Milton, God re-

---

51   Ibid.
52   Ibid.
53   Ibid., p. 61.
54   Ibid.
55   Ibid.

vealed himself first to the English; in contrast, Michelet suggests that humanity has followed a journey with truth appearing in a fragmentary form, in Asia, then in Europe, in England, in Germany, and in Italy, up until the moment France reveals this truth to the whole world. Why is France accorded this privilege? Because France is the nation in which 'the social people' takes form — that is, the people in whom the different races have come together. As he writes, 'Once this order has been felt in the limited society of one's own country, the same idea will spread to human society, to the republic of the world.'[56]

It would be wrong to think that Michelet neglects the work of might in the establishment of right. He emphasizes France's action and describes its 'love of conquest', but at the same time asserts that it is only 'The pretext of our wars', 'For proselytism is the more ardent motive.'[57] The French have the power of universal assimilation, which he defines as 'an assimilation of minds, a conquering of wills', leaving no doubt as to the convergence of these two aspects: 'Every one of our armies, withdrawing, has left behind a France.'[58] In his words, the people of France are 'the legislative people of modern times, as Rome was the legislative people of antiquity.'[59] He adds: 'France acts and reasons, decrees and does battle; she shakes the world, makes history and recounts it.'[60] It is difficult not to discern the signs of a religious mission in her past. The idea of the translation of heaven to earth does not mean that God was a fiction created by humankind in order to mask their temporary inability to assume their task down here. If that were the

---

56   Ibid.
57   Ibid., p. 51.
58   Ibid.
59   Ibid.
60   Ibid., p. 52.

case, Michelet would not speak of the unity of humanity in a divine society. And he would not, at the same time, declare:

> If a social sense is to lead us back to religion, then the organ of that new revelation, the interpreter between God and man, should be the most social of all peoples. The moral world received its Word in Christianity, the child of Judea and of Greece; France will explain the Word of the social world that we now see beginning.[61]

Far from breaking with the language of the theologico-political, Michelet goes so far as to speak of a 'pontificate of the new civilization', which the peoples discern in France, 'by their silent imitation at least'.[62]

Michelet will never renounce the idea of France and of the social people which he formed in the work of his youth. Nonetheless, in his *History of the French Revolution* he will develop an understanding of the monarchy which breaks with his earlier views (largely under Guizot's influence). To my mind, it is telling that this change is accompanied by an explicit reference to Dante. Right at the start of the second part of his introduction, entitled 'On the Old Monarchy', he writes:

> As early as the year 1300, I behold the great Ghibelin poet, who, in opposition to the pope, strengthens and exalts to heaven the Colossus of Caesar. *Unity* is salvation; *one* monarch for the whole earth. Then, blindly following up his austere, inflexible logic, he lays it down, that the greater this monarch, the more he becomes omnipotent,

---

61   Ibid., p. 61. [Translator's note: Here Lefort actually misquotes Michelet, replacing 'l'organe' with 'l'origine'.]

62   Ibid., p. 62.

— the more he becomes a God, the less mankind must fear the abuse of his power. If he has all, he desires nought; still less can he envy or hate. He is perfect, and perfectly, sovereignly just; he governs infallibly, like the justice of God.

Such is the ground-work of all the theories which have since been heaped up in support of this principle: *Unity*, and the supposed result of unity, *peace*. And since then we have hardly ever had anything but wars.

We must dig lower than Dante, and discover and look into the earth for the deep popular foundation whereon the Colossus was built.[63]

Michelet continues immediately:

Man needs justice. A captive within the straight limits of a dogma reposing entirely on the arbitrary grace of God, he thought to save justice in a political religion, and made unto himself, of a man, a *God of Justice*, hoping that this visible God would preserve for him the light of equity which had been darkened in the other.[64]

I needed this long quotation because it calls for some commentary. Michelet finds in Dante's work the foundation of all the theories erected in support of national monarchies. And this foundation is the principle of unity. However, his criticism implies a self-criticism, since in the *Introduction to World History* he attributes to the French monarchy the merit of having, through its work of levelling out, contributed wonderfully to the formation of the unity of the people. The signs in this work which I ascribed to Dante's

---

63   Jules Michelet, *History of the French Revolution*, ed. by Gordon Wright, trans. by Charles Cocks (Chicago, IL: University of Chicago Press, 1967), p. 41.

64   Ibid.

inspiration seemed convincing to me. Need I add that in the pages where Michelet celebrates Italy's own genius, Dante is mentioned four times? Michelet's dialogue with Dante thus seems to have been carried out over a long period of time. Finally, I would note that, while Michelet attributes to Dante the origin of the modern theory of monarchy, and more generally that of salvation through unity, he does not break with him. If that had been the case, what would the words 'We must dig lower than Dante' mean? Michelet tacitly recognizes that Dante to his credit sought the means of conceiving Justice on earth, even though he considers Dante to have missed his aim. As is very evident, Michelet moves directly from Dante to humankind: 'Man needs justice. [...] [H]e thought to save justice in a political religion.'[65] In this manner Michelet suggests that Dante shared a general belief. It was not only his 'austere, inflexible logic', which he followed 'blindly'; he was also blindly wedded to the collective faith which leads to investing divine justice in the power of one alone.

Michelet's attachment to Dante is, moreover, evident in the text which he places at the start of Book III of his *History* ('On the Method and Spirit of this Book').[66] At one point, he opposes 'simple' and 'clever' people, the latter 'guileful individuals' who act like 'friends of the people' but who, in fact, despise the people and claim to judge the Revolution from the heights of their learning. Now, he grants to those 'simple' people illustrious forebears, citing three names: Dante, Shakespeare, and Luther. He writes

---

65   Ibid.

66   [Translator's note: This prefatory text, from the start of volume 2 of Michelet's *History of the French Revolution*, is not included in Cocks's translation, and so the subsequent quotations from Michelet in this paragraph are my own translation. The phrase 'guileful individuals' translates the tricky phrase 'gens d'esprit'.]

that these three bent down in front of the people, in order to 'gather up and write their words'. He adds that it was 'the people whom Dante came to hear in the marketplace of Florence'. It is true that if we compare these two statements, it has to be admitted that they are in disagreement. Both suggest that Dante is a spokesperson for the people, but the second one argues that the judgement of the people is essentially right, whereas the first indicates that, swept along by their desire for justice, the people create their own servitude, and that the Ghibelline poet, by echoing this desire, unintentionally lays the foundations for domination. The ambiguous nature of Michelet's relationship with Dante is connected to Michelet's own ambiguous relationship with the people.

If I were interested in Michelet for his own sake, I could easily demonstrate that, in his *History of the Revolution*, neither the acute sense he acquires of the creation of a political religion under the Ancien Régime, nor his effort to penetrate the 'mystery of monarchical incarnation' make him renounce his religious vision of France's role in the history of humanity. He translates the idea of unity and sovereignty which he pursues in visible things into the realm of things invisible. For instance, seduced by Mirabeau's phrase, he declares that the Law is the sovereign of the world. He speaks of the return of Justice, as if she had fled the earth. He evokes the advent of the royalty of the spirit, recognizes the Revolution as a new religion, and describes the revolutionary war as sacred. For him, the Festival of the Federation is the 'union of France with France', and this marital union seems to him to be 'a prophetic symbol of the future alliance of nations, of the general marriage of the world'.[67] To all those who witnessed this

---

67　Ibid., p. 454.

event, he attributes the following exclamation: "'Ah! if I were *one*," says the world; "if I could at length unite my scattered members, and bring my nations together!'"[68] Finally, bringing together the hope of each individual with the unity of the human race, he concludes: 'This ever impotent desire both of the world and the human soul, a nation seemed to be realising at that fugitive hour, playing that *divine comedy* of union and concord which we never behold but in our dreams.'[69] Who could doubt but that Dante's thought continues to haunt him? The persistence of that which is ours only in our dreams is for him an indication of the life of the spirit and of the imprint of the divine in humans. Does not Michelet declare: 'A strange *vita nuova*, one eminently spiritual, and making her whole Revolution a sort of dream, at one time delightful, at another terrible, is now beginning for France. It knew neither time nor space.'?[70]

Michelet seems to me to be an exemplary witness. On the one hand, he effectuates an extraordinary transposition of the ideal of the *Monarchia* by assigning universal jurisdiction to France and by bestowing religious meaning on the people and on humanity. On the other hand, he discovers a political religion which came in answer to the expectations of the people and was able to keep them for a long time in servitude. His thinking moves in two directions which are contrary but not alien to one another. In the Revolution he finds something other than the transformation of property relations, or the solution to what others call 'the social question'. He sees the birth of faith in humanity, a faith which does not break with God but which

---

68   Ibid., p. 456.

69   Ibid. [Lefort's emphasis].

70   Ibid., p. 444.

relinquishes the illusion of the impossibility of salvation on earth and grants to every individual the will to ensure the spreading of justice by their works. The symbol of the Revolution, in July 1790, is living: 'This symbol for man is man. All the conventional world crumbling to pieces, a holy respect possesses him for the true image of God.'[71] If this is the heart of the matter, Michelet must reject the idea that, for centuries, people have been subjected to an external power raining down upon them, or, equally, that their ordeals were but the result of the painful birth of the nation. Belief must be the key to the Ancien Régime, as it is to the Revolution. Michelet has to admit that the people subjugated themselves by projecting the image of their unity in a prince and by making of that prince the sovereign judge. Let us repeat the injunction: *we must dig lower than Dante.* Humanity only becomes conscious of its quest for itself when it has ceased to worship the *one* in some *other* which is separate from all.

DANTE AND LA BOÉTIE

Michelet seems to me to be an exemplary witness, because his work brings together two contrary inclinations which had previously appeared to be separate: on the one hand, the tendency, whether deliberate or not, to use parts of the picture of the *Monarchia* to shape events which announce the conclusion of the drama of humanity; on the other hand, the habit of taking from this work the principle on which domination relies and of deriving from the refutation of this principle a new conception of the political. Michelet's transformation, however singular, of universal monarchy into a world republic led by France fits into the

---

71   Ibid., p. 445.

pattern that I have sketched out. But it must also be admitted that Michelet was not the first to consider that the monarch's power exerts a force of attraction on his subjects, and that his subjects consent to their subjection. This idea emerged at a time when Florentine humanists were defending the republican form of government and seeking the reasons for the advent of Caesar in the degradation of the people. It is most fully developed in Étienne de La Boétie's *Discourse of Voluntary Servitude*. Did Michelet read this work (reissued by Lammenais in 1835)? Was it this work that taught him the need to dig lower than Dante? I cannot guarantee that this is the case, but the image he puts forward in the phrase over which I paused can already be found in La Boétie, and I find it difficult to believe that this is sheer coincidence. At the point when the author calls on those peoples who are enslaved to a tyrant, he writes:

> I do not ask that you place hands upon the tyrant to topple him over, but simply that you support him no longer; then you will behold him, *like a great Colossus whose pedestal has been pulled away*, fall of his own weight and break into pieces.[72]

The *Discourse* was known under the title *Against One*. This title is well deserved, even though it was given to the text by polemicists serving the Reformation. They granted it a circulation which its author did not desire. We know that Montaigne liked it so much that he wanted to publish it in the middle of his *Essais*, and that he gave up on this project precisely for fear of abetting the designs of the Protestants. Montaigne knew his friend better than anyone else.

---

72   Étienne de La Boétie, *Anti-Dictator: The 'Discours sur la servitude volontaire' of Étienne de La Boétie, Rendered into English*, trans. by Harry Kurz (New York: Columbia University Press, 1942), pp. 12–13. [Lefort's emphasis; hereafter cited as *Discourse*.]

Moreover, the *Memoir on the Pacification of the Troubles*, written a few years after the *Discourse*, leaves no doubt as to the intentions of its author; he wanted the Catholic religion to be stripped of all the pomp contrary to its nature, but he did not want the king to consent to the coexistence of two equally legitimate religions.[73] Nonetheless, the *Discourse* is undoubtedly topical, taking this term in its broadest sense.[74] It attacks both the monarchies of its day and the beliefs which they inspired. There are many indications which suggest that reading Dante shed light for La Boétie on the origin of the evils of monarchical power, and that he wanted to overturn Dante's argument.

The *Discourse* begins with words from Homer, voiced by Ulysses: 'No good thing is a multitude of lords; let there be one lord, one king.'[75] It will be recalled that Dante invoked this same quotation, placing it under the authority of Aristotle. La Boétie uses it for a different purpose: 'he should have maintained that the rule of several could not be good since the power of one man alone, as soon as he acquires the title of master, becomes abusive and unreasonable.'[76] A few lines later, he rewords his analysis:

> Yet, in the light of reason, it is a great misfortune to be at the beck and call of one master, for it is impossible to be sure that he is going to be kind, since it is always in his power to be cruel whenever he pleases.[77]

---

73   See Étienne de La Boétie, *Mémoire sur la pacification des troubles*, ed. by Malcolm Smith (Geneva: Droz, 1983).

74   [Translator's note: The term that Lefort uses here is 'l'actualité du *Discours*'.]

75   Homer, *Iliad*, i, p. 77 (ii, vv. 204–05).

76   La Boétie, *Discourse*, p. 39.

77   Ibid., p. 40.

The emperor's power is not mentioned, nor is the fact that people have been ruled by several monarchs. The author's target is the master, wherever he appears, for his image always bears the mark of redoubtable power. La Boétie names a tyrant whoever holds this power, and there is no doubt that every monarch is a tyrant. In the course of his argument, he observes at one point: 'There are three kinds of tyrants; some receive their proud position through elections by the people, others by force of arms, others by inheritance.'[78] Having noted some differences between the three, he concludes:

> still the method of ruling is practically the same; those who are elected act as if they were breaking in bullocks; those who are conquerors make the people their prey; those who are heirs plan to treat them as if they were their natural slaves.[79]

The distinction between lawful and unlawful princes thus proves to be meaningless. In any case, from the very beginning of the text, the author is careful to point out that his aim is not to consider, in the wake of many others, 'whether other types of government are preferable to monarchy'.[80] He continues:

> still I should like to know, before casting doubt on the place that monarchy should occupy among commonwealths, whether or not it belongs to such a group, since it is hard to believe that there is anything of common wealth in a country where everything belongs to one master.[81]

---

78   Ibid., p. 52.
79   Ibid., p. 53.
80   Ibid., p. 40.
81   Ibid.

Dante, having stated the subject of his research as politics, that is, the source and principle of rightful constitutions, immediately transgresses the traditional framework in order to establish the legitimacy of universal monarchy. Similarly, La Boétie loses interest in the conventional classification of different forms of government, but does so, however, in order to demonstrate the evil hidden in monarchy, whatever the form or reach of its jurisdiction. Dante and La Boétie both get to the heart of the matter, asking: what is the foundation of the power of *one alone*?

In Dante's treatise, the monarch's power derives directly from the position which he occupies, alone above all. Unlike other authors before him, Dante considers neither how the monarch should govern, nor his qualities, nor his education. Once the monarch has no rival, he is thereby freed from all covetousness, and in a way forced to wish for what is good. La Boétie is similarly audacious in his analysis, arguing that such is the position of the monarch that he is able to be wicked whenever he likes. Dante is not concerned about cases of bad emperors; the example of Nero, for instance, has nothing to teach him. La Boétie, for his part, does note in passing that 'the inhabitants of a country' may happen to confer government on a wise and valiant man who deserves their esteem and trust, and, albeit not without some reservation, he concedes that it would be undesirable to get rid of such a man.[82] Yet this sort of obedience stems, we learn, from the 'duties of human relationship'.[83] In short, people respond to the good things they have received with a feeling of gratitude and veneration. There is no political lesson to be learnt from this example.

---

82   Ibid., p. 41.
83   Ibid.

However, the extent of their opposition to one another cannot be measured by considering only the way in which each judges the monarch's power. If, for Dante, the emperor's power is essentially good, this is because it stems from the unification of the human race and is, at the same time, an agent of that unification. The individual has their own particular goal, as does each family, village, city, and kingdom; only humanity has its goal in itself. As is evident in nature, the existence of the whole explains the *raison-d'être* of each of its constituent parts. Consideration of the human body confirms the truth of this principle, since any organ or limb can only be defined in relation to the task which it carries out on behalf of the end pursued by 'the whole person'. It is this principle of the organic constitution of human society which La Boétie attacks. In so doing, there is no better example for La Boétie's argument than tyranny, as it is commonly presented. Tyranny proves to be very revealing. Effectively, since the system of government which is considered to be the most corrupt is formed or maintained by the cooperation of those whom it oppresses, its power must be driven by a certain charm, that of the name of the one alone. The first question asked by La Boétie thus assumes its full meaning in comparison to Dante's theory:

> For the present I should like merely to understand how it happens that *so many men, so many villages, so many cities, so many nations*, sometimes suffer under a single tyrant who has no other power than the power they give him; who is able to harm them only to the extent to which they have the willingness to bear with him; who could do them absolutely no injury unless they preferred to put up with him rather than contradict him. Surely a striking situation! Yet it is so common that one must grieve the more and wonder the less at the spectacle of

> a million men serving in wretchedness, their necks
> under the yoke, not constrained by a greater multi-
> tude than they, but simply, it would seem, delighted
> and charmed by the name of one man alone.[84]

What did Dante, in his day, view as a consequence of the rejection of the authority of the emperor? The misfortune of division. La Boétie, meanwhile, lays out the spectacle of different peoples, each one subject to a tyrant whom they not only serve but also want to be their master, and who will accept any form of suffering rather than raise their voice against him. They do not give in to his power, nor are they entranced by his person. La Boétie writes that people will give up their most precious possessions, their life even, in order to serve not a Hercules or a Samson, but rather 'a single little man', 'Too frequently [...] the most cowardly and effeminate in the nation'.[85] It is the charm of the name of the one alone which captivates, and it is this charm which is to be blamed for the misfortunes of the times. I noted that according to Dante the trials by combat fought by claimants to the supreme power in Antiquity had helped the progress of humanity towards its unity and that henceforth, this unity having been revealed, the reign of the emperor was no longer reliant on conquest; clear assent to his authority from the peoples sufficed to turn right into reality. La Boétie, who calls the monarch a tyrant, does not think that war should be waged against him:

> Obviously there is no need of fighting to overcome
> this single tyrant, for he is automatically defeated if
> the country refuses consent to its own enslavement:

---

84   Ibid., pp. 40–41 [Lefort's emphasis].

85   Ibid., p. 42.

> it is not necessary to deprive him of anything, but simply to give him nothing.[86]

According to the author of the *Monarchia*, consent is all that is required for the master to become omnipotent; according to the author of the *Discourse*, withholding this consent is all that is required for the master to forgo his omnipotence. However effective the emperor's actions are deemed to be, for the benefit (argues the former) or misfortune (argues the latter) of all, his authority is above all symbolic. Thus everything suggests that La Boétie knew Dante's argument and understood it very well.

From Dante La Boétie takes the idea that the emperor makes the name of the one resound in all places and that humanity in this way understands itself as one. But for La Boétie, this idea gives credence to an illusion, which is at the heart of the strange phenomenon that is voluntary servitude. The name of the one deafens the prince's subjects and makes them mute. If they would rather suffer him than contradict him, it seems that this is because he rescues them from the risk of having to understand one another, of having to talk to one another, of having to experience ceaselessly the differences between each other. If they give in to the charm of the name of the one alone, is this not because uncertainty is inextricable from their condition of having the gift of language? In fact, there is a moment when, invoking Nature and the gift of language which she has given to us, La Boétie seems to reveal his thought most clearly. In his words, what is most evident is that 'nature, handmaiden of God, governess of men, has cast us all in the same mold in order that we may behold in one another

---

86   Ibid., p. 44.

companions, or rather brothers'.[87] Then, having acknow-
ledged that people do not enjoy the same advantages, he
continues:

> Hence, since this kind mother has given us the
> whole world as a dwelling place, has lodged us in
> the same house, has fashioned us according to the
> same model so that in beholding one another we
> might almost recognize ourselves; since she has
> bestowed upon us all the great gift of voice and
> speech for fraternal relationship, thus achieving by
> the common and mutual statement of our thoughts
> a communion of our wills; and since she has tried
> in every way to narrow and tighten the bond of our
> union and kinship; since she has revealed in every
> possible manner her intention, not so much to asso-
> ciate us as to make us one organic whole, there can
> be no further doubt that we are all naturally free.[88]

All these fine-tuned turns of phrase deserve to be under-
scored for how well they bring out the need not to separate
these two ideas: on the one hand, that humans have the
same provenance, are related, and share the same earth; on
the other hand, that they are irreducibly distinct. The same
natural inclination leads them to live together and to live as
individuals.

In this way, the extent to which La Boétie distances
himself from Dante is clear. He suggests that humanity
is one, but that this unity can neither be imagined nor
achieved outside of the ties which people and communi-
ties establish with one other. The visible sign of union is
deceptive: in truth, nature has made us *not so much all*

---

87   Ibid., p. 50.
88   Ibid.

united as all ones.[89] However, individuals only discover themselves as ones through the relationship which they establish with those with whom they share their life. Accordingly, it is not in the monarch that everyone is reflected; rather, people recognize themselves as alike by accepting their differences as they gaze at their reflection in one another. These are not the alternatives described by Dante: union or division; incorporation into the great whole or fragmentation. The communion of wills assumes the mutual declaration of thoughts, and not the abdication of thought in front of him whose will is law. Does La Boétie not suggest that the charm of one name alone (the author deliberately does not say the name of one alone) works because it responds to people's desire to hear themselves named and to have the need to name each other assuaged? And that this name finally springs up, not from each person taken individually, but rather as a consequence of their passionate proximity?

Moreover, the *Discourse* offers the best explanation of the origin of the charm, when it adds to the power of the name, which renders the word meaningless, the power of the image, which makes each person lose the ability to see that which is before their very eyes. In the passage already mentioned in which he addresses unhappy peoples, the author remarks:

> He who thus domineers over you has only two eyes, only two hands, only one body, no more than is possessed by the least man among the infinite numbers dwelling in your cities; he has indeed nothing more than the power that you confer upon him to destroy you. Where has he acquired enough eyes to spy

---

89   [Translator's note: see Judith Revel's essay in this volume for discussion of this phrase, which plays on the contrast in the original French between 'unis' and 'uns'.]

> upon you, if you do not provide them yourselves?
> How can he have so many arms to beat you with, if
> he does not borrow them from you? The feet that
> trample down your cities, where does he get them
> if they are not your own? How does he have any
> power over you except through you?[90]

Reading these lines, we once more remember one of Dante's key themes. The conception of a body politic which would be represented by an omnipotent, omniscient, and as if omnipresent monarch seems, to La Boétie, to be the translation of a fantasy. In reality, there are only bodies which are equally singular and equally limited. And the fantasy hides a body that is itself also singular, but which, as a result of this fantasy, gains the power to dominate those who created this fantasy, turning against them their own sight and strength. This analysis goes quite far since it encourages the detection of the lie that may be contained in the slogan 'to die for one's country'. In effect, La Boétie praises the Athenians, the Spartans, and the Romans who sacrificed their life for their city, but emphasizes that in so doing they were defending their freedom. In contrast, the subjects who 'go bravely to war' and do not hesitate to 'offer [their] own bodies unto death' have been carried away by the aforementioned fantasy.[91]

The *Discourse* goes against Dante and, at the same time, as I have noted, it also goes against the cult of monarchy in its own day, especially in France. Its author was a contemporary of Guillaume Postel, a celebrated theorist of French imperial monarchy (*Les Raisons de la monarchie* [*Reasons for Monarchy*] dates from 1551). He was also a contemporary of the Pléiade poets, including most notably Du

---

90   Ibid., p. 46.
91   Ibid.

Bellay and Ronsard. At one point, La Boétie mentions the latter with ironical reverence, hinting at the amusement that the composition of the *Franciade* provokes in him. He understands the function of the Trojan myth, and of the symbols that the humanists took from the ancient world, but he also appreciates the role played by religion. Having noted that this last — religion — served the ancient tyrants as a 'cloak', he writes that 'Our own leaders have employed in France certain similar devices, such as toads, fleurs-de-lys, sacred vessels, and standards with flames of gold'.[92] Nowhere in his work do we encounter any allusion to the intervention of providence nor to the theory of a chosen people. The example of Israel, which gave itself a tyrant 'without any compulsion or need',[93] distresses him; how much more distressing must he have found the example of nations who have been subjugated for centuries and who believe that empire is their vocation.

It remains certain that La Boétie, despite his criticism of its principles, maintained a close connection with Dante's political humanism, and that this connection is not to be found in the zealous advocates of modern monarchies who sought inspiration in Dante's treatise. The author of the *Discourse* seeks in his turn to give to political life its full dignity, and to decipher the traits of *humanitas* in *civilitas*. This last remark brings me back to Dante. In my analysis of his treatise, I have tried to bring out its ambiguity. The sovereign that he imagines undoubtedly appears to be omnipotent, a fact which justifies the image of the Colossus before whom everyone bows. However, the sovereign's authority is essentially symbolic, and the human race does not find itself condemned to uniformity

---

92   Ibid., p. 68.
93   Ibid., p. 53.

under his reign. Each people is meant to live in peace, keeping their own customs and obeying the laws which are right for them. The Asian or African peoples are no less part of humanity — without them being expected to convert to Christianity — than the Romans or the Germans. Neither La Boétie nor Michelet can entirely break free from Dante.

If Dante's oeuvre helps us to understand the links which have been established in support of a new idea of sovereignty, between universalism, imperialism, and nationalism, it also encourages us, if not to undo these links, at least to disentangle them in order to examine his *work*, knowing *how to use time.*

TRANSLATED FROM THE FRENCH BY
JENNIFER RUSHWORTH

Lefort/Dante
Reading, Misreading, Transforming
JUDITH REVEL

In recent years, I have become very interested in Claude
Lefort from the point of view of contemporary philosophy
— more particularly, contemporary political philosophy
and contemporary representations of history, which are
the two areas of enquiry with which my own work is concerned. It is therefore from this specific vantage point —
both situated and defending its evident subjectivity — that
I will suggest some points for reflection based on Dante's
Monarchia and Claude Lefort's reading of that same text.
Accordingly, this vantage point, which is that of a reader,
and is therefore subject to all the biases which inform
every act of reading, also includes the ways in which Lefort
himself misreads Dante's text and in so doing makes it so
excitingly complex. Every reading, however philological, is
an exercise in cutting up and reinvention. Lefort does not
have any philological aspirations, and nor — much more
modestly, nearly a quarter of a century later — do I. Rather,

we share the intention to bring a text to life by making it one's own, probably by misreading and transforming it, and by making the questions that it formulates and the proposals that it puts forward resonate in the present. 'We must digest what we read; otherwise it will merely enter the memory and not the reasoning power',[1] writes Seneca to Lucilius on the subject of the exercise of recollecting, remembering, and ordering things read which make up the *hypomnemata*. The brief essay in *reading a reading* — reading the reading that Lefort so brilliantly offers us of Dante — which I would like to undertake here has no other aim than that outlined by Seneca: namely, the modest digestion of two potent subject matters, embedded one within the other, the Dantean material and its Lefortian re-elaboration.

The first point which I would like to address as a way into Lefort's reading is methodological in nature, and concerns precisely the question of reading, that is, the question of what we mean by *reading a text*. Part of the purpose of this point is likely that of protecting Lefort from eventual criticisms which medievalists or Dante specialists — note that Lefort is neither of these — might otherwise level against him. Nonetheless, the 'defensive' nature of this point should not prevent us from understanding that it also corresponds to a serious challenge on the part of Lefort, and one which he puts into practice in his reading of Dante just as in his reading of Machiavelli, or in his reading of texts by Marx. This challenge consists in affirming a mode of reading that is rooted *in the present,* and aims in a way to enact a return to the present. This mode of reading

1   Seneca, *Epistles*, trans. by Richard M. Gunmere, 3 vols (Cambridge, MA: Harvard University Press, 1996–2001), ii (2001), p. 281 (from Letter 84) [translation amended].

is proposed not *in place of* a philological reading that all of us very often practise in relation to 'our' authors or to the corpus of texts which we confront, but rather *alongside*, or *in addition to* that reading approach.

When he justifies theoretically the principle of such a presentist mode of reading, Lefort paradoxically articulates it in terms of the importance of a historicizing gesture which is, for him, never able to be renounced. Now, historicization paradoxically implies the development of two approaches which are both distinct and complementary: on the one hand, the restitution and analysis of past systems of thought (in the case with which we are concerned, this particular system of thought is itself rooted in other systems of thought, starting with the Aristotelian notion of the 'possible intellect', which is a key focal point for much of Lefort's commentary, but also including 'the writings of important Christian authors',[2] from Augustine to Thomas Aquinas); on the other hand, the concomitant, constantly reaffirmed desire to situate oneself in relation to one's own present, because the present cannot be grasped in its specificity save in the play of oppositions and continuities, whether partial or total, which qualify it as such.

The present can thus be understood through a process of differentiation, on the basis of what it no longer, or no longer entirely, is. But it can also be understood through the effects of continuity and the echoes elicited by the description of a former time, that is, a scene of past thought which seems on the surface radically different. In a historical, philosophical, political landscape, there one day arose a particular inaugural moment, a sort of moment of emergence — Lefort speaks of 'an immense step beyond

---

2   Lefort, 'Dante's Modernity', in this volume, pp. 1–85 (p. 3).

the field of ancient philosophy'.[3] It is this novelty which needs to be located and analysed, which is also its own 'germination', what has come down to us, seven centuries later. Precisely because in our own time its belated echo can still perhaps be heard. 'Dante's modernity', since that is the title of the essay by Lefort which accompanies the text of the *Monarchia*, as a consequence includes both his status as a point of rupture and his ability to talk, even today, about us.

Lefort briefly cites Kantorowicz — Chapter VIII of *The King's Two Bodies*, 'Man-centered Kingship: Dante'[4] — in the opening pages of his own essay, and comments:

> Dante shows himself to be so dependent on the knowledge and language of his time that the reader can easily overlook the 'slant so new and so surprising' that he gives to all the statements that he has borrowed and miss his intention and the new solutions that he offers.[5]

If this is the difficulty, Lefort also makes the wager that

> we should be less concerned about failing to grasp the full extent of his borrowings — through lack of the competences of the historian or the theologian — or of the use he makes of the debates about the relations between religion and philosophy. For in this case our confidence in the vigour of his thought, or, to use an image dear to Dante, its fecundity, is only increased.[6]

---

3   Ibid., p. 6.

4   'Man-Centered Kingship: Dante', in Ernst H. Kantorowicz, *The King's Two Bodies: A Study in Mediaeval Political Theology* (Princeton, NJ: Princeton University Press, 1997), pp. 451–95.

5   Lefort, 'Dante's Modernity', p. 7.

6   Ibid., pp. 7–8.

The principle of reading is as a result largely redefined, because there is no political analysis — whether it concerns an author (Machiavelli) or a text (in this case, the *Monarchia*) — without the central importance of an inquiry into the present; but there is also no conflation of these two 'times', which reading brings into tension, into a totality tasked with revealing their truth. Any ambiguity can be resolved by going back to the extraordinary opening essay of the first issue of the journal *Libre*, founded by Lefort and others in 1977[7] — an article whose title, 'Now', also sounds in itself like a declaration of intent:

> That the historical dimension must be rescued along with the political dimension does not mean that we want to restore a theory of universal history. We reject the viewpoint that stands over and above the social totality as well as the vision of the becoming of humanity as a self-generating evolution or succession of 'formations'. We also reject the notion of a substance called 'Society' and that of a full time or of a continuum of meaning. The term 'historical dimension' is advanced precisely in order to avoid the equivocation attached to the idea of history; in order to suggest that there is no way of understanding the manifestations of social reality in the present which does not also presume their apprehension in time [...]. This means that modern society (in the plural) cannot be placed into history like an actor's gestures and words are placed at the proper moment in the plot. Modern society must be known in its historicity, through events that are not simply constellations of accidents but which are shaped by modern society, thus revealing its relation to change, a style

---

7   Lefort, 'Maintenant', *Libre*, 1 (1977), pp. 3–28, English as 'Then and Now', trans. by Dick Howard, Jean Cohen, Patricia Tummons, Mark Poster, and Andrew Arato, *Telos: A Quarterly Journal of Radical Thought*, 36 (1978), pp. 29–42.

> of discriminating past and future — or an inability
> to fall back wholly on acquired knowledge or an
> excessiveness which is conducive to the test of
> what invalidates it.[8]

What this means is that if interest in the present is not enclosed within the narrow confines of a presentist approach which forgets both the sedimentary thickness of its own ground and the horizon of projects to come (I am thinking here of the recent analyses of François Hartog, to which Lefort's approach does not seem to correspond at all),[9] this same interest does nonetheless imply something like 'a style of discriminating past and future', or, in other words, the identification of moments of transformation and change, entirely freed from a totalizing vision and yet entirely effective.

What the present enables us to think, and what the historicization of the enquiry — whether it is philosophical, philological, political, or sociological — gives us the means to understand, is the specificity of a configuration which is both produced by its own historical conditions (which need to be described) and irreducible to an overarching interpretation given in advance. The insistent commentary that Lefort provides of the notion of *civilitas* is an excellent example of this: 'let us not be afraid to translate this as civil society', notes Lefort.[10] In this note, we have both a record of what Lefort identifies as the novelty of Dante (since human society exceeds the restricted limits of Aristotelian community) and, at the same time, the connecting thread which emerges between *civilitas* and *humanitas* — in other

---

8   Lefort, 'Then and Now', pp. 41–42 [translation amended].

9   François Hartog, *Regimes of Historicity: Presentism and Experiences of Time*, trans. by Saskia Brown (New York: Columbia University Press, 2015).

10   Lefort, 'Dante's Modernity', p. 4.

words, according to Lefort, the relinquishing of a Thomist vision of humanity understood on the grounds of the idea of original sin, and its replacement by the positivity of a collective effort at the realization of humankind's humanity, the secularization of the Christian idea of universal community, and the echo, so to speak in advance, of the modern representation of a community of the human race.

One last point in this rather long introduction devoted to what is meant by *reading*. The necessary historicization of the investigation that we undertake at a particular moment — since 1312 is neither 1993, the date of publication of Lefort's text, nor is it 2019, our own present moment — is in reality also what gives us the greatest freedom in our use of the authors that we mobilize. Not because the art of commentary would suddenly be freed from its fundamental concern of respect for the text or its literal meaning, but rather because every single thought is produced in a context which shapes it and which that thought in turn helps to elucidate. It is in discussing his relationship to Marx that Lefort is most explicit about this strange gesture that constitutes *reading*:

> No matter what help one can derive from commentators, to read Marx is to question him (an effort that today is becoming increasingly difficult, it is true). This freedom requires one: to accept the indeterminacy that accompanies the movement of writing; to test its gaps, its new beginnings in subsequent texts; to be willing to discover a thought being worked on by what it grasps, to let oneself be led to what it grasps; to let oneself thus be drawn to the questions that made Marx speak, questions which he made prominent and which are not concealed by his answers, since it is not a matter of problems and solutions. And the liberty that is so gained increases with the very reading, *which leads*

> *readers to confront their own time, that which they, in turn, must grasp in their own place, now.*[11]

If we replace Marx's name with Dante's, it seems to me that this passage offers us the key to Lefortian commentary:

> [...] to let oneself thus be drawn to the questions that made *Dante* speak, questions which he made prominent and which are not concealed by his answers, since it is not a matter of problems and solutions. And the liberty that is so gained increases with the very reading, *which leads readers to confront their own time, that which they, in turn, must grasp in their own place, now.*

This extraordinary lesson in reading contains at least two important elements. The first is that at the heart of the act of reading there is no intention of obtaining from the text anything like an immutable truth, the truth-of-the-text-and-its-author, because the only truth that can be found therein is the patient effort of writing which accompanied the work of thought of which the writing took charge. To call this 'indeterminacy', as Lefort does, does not mean that a text, precisely because it is indeterminate, would be endowed with a universal value, would all of a sudden erase its context, the process and eventual errancies of its own constitution, and could suddenly go forth under the auspices of its own truth — let us recall Althusser's 'scientific' Marx, against which the Lefortian method seems here openly to take a stance. 'Indeterminacy' is quite the opposite, and means situating thought once more in the context of its effort and its tensions, that is to say also in the context of its own history; it means analysing its determinations, and at the same time feeling free to confront afresh, in its wake, in

---

11 Lefort, 'Then and Now', p. 32. Emphasis added [translation amended].

the very same gesture, *one's own time* — a time which does not need to affirm the literal, identical repetition of what was in reality the time of Marx, or the time of Machiavelli, or the time of Dante... — but which is committed quite simply, as Lefort says, to *confronting one's own time* and grasping what one designates precisely as 'now'.

I would like now to suggest a few points where we see this double aspect of reading: situating thought once more within the context of its effort and its tensions, grasping its novelty, of course; but also putting its propositions literally to work in our own time, and seeing what they tell us about ourselves.

I will highlight two such moments in particular, both of which essentially relate to Book I of the *Monarchia*. The first point, which is central for Dante, and whose potency Lefort develops, concerns the reference to the *possible intellect*; beyond Lefort, I will propose an interpretation of the *possible intellect* in terms of the constitution of the common of human beings.[12] The second, which is more Lefortian but which is in a way projected by Lefort onto Dante's

---

12   [Translator's note: As Michael Hardt and Antonio Negri note in their preface to *Multitude: War and Democracy in the Age of Empire* (New York, NY: The Penguin Press, 2004), the notion of 'the common' is 'more awkward' than that of 'the commons', but also signals a new development with a different philosophical content (p. xv). The article by Judith Revel and Antonio Negri, 'Inventer le commun des hommes', *Multitudes*, 31.4 (2007), pp. 5–10 <https://doi.org/10.3917/mult.031.0005> was translated as 'Inventing the Common' (2008) <http://www.generation-online.org/p/fp_revel5.htm> [accessed 8 December 2019]. A key term in Michael Hardt and Antonio Negri, *Commonwealth* (Cambridge, MA: Belknap, 2009), the notion of the common has since also appeared in book titles, including Pierre Dadot and Christian Laval, *Commun: Essai sur la révolution au XXIe siècle* (Paris: La Découverte, 2014), English as *Common: On Revolution in the 21st Century* (London: Bloomsbury, 2019) and, most recently, *L'Alternative du commun*, ed. by Christian Laval, Pierre Sauvêtre, and Ferhat Taylan (Paris: Hermann, 2019).]

text, is the very complicated question of the One, in other words, the difficulty of claiming simultaneously the coherence, cohesion, and power of a collective intellect reliant upon the idea that in reality humanity has no outside, that humanity is made up of heterogeneous peoples who are sometimes opposed, and at other times unaware of each other, but all of whom contribute to the progressive realization of the knowledgeable nature of the human race, on the one hand; and, on the other hand (this is the other side of this difficult simultaneity), what Lefort has always clung to as a fundamental point of his analysis, that is, the fact that the One, when it involves self-identity, the suppression of differences, and the erasure of conflicts, is politically death-bringing, and represents, putting it in modern terms, the always possible turning-point of democracy into its opposite. All this immediately begs a question: is it possible to construct an idea of universality which would not immediately mean affirmation of the One? Dante is here an invaluable guide, precisely because the *Monarchia* develops the idea of a cooperative universality, or rather redefines universality not as the ground for human community but rather as what human cooperation is liable to constitute, and accordingly reverses the logical order: universality is an *effect* of cooperation, and not its condition of possibility. In any case, this — and I will return to this point momentarily — seems to me to be what fascinates Lefort about Dante: the possibility of a universality without the One.

Let's take the first of these two points: the astonishing adoption and re-elaboration of the Aristotelian theme of the *possible intellect*. I will discuss this theme quite quickly and do not want to insist on aspects that are well known — Dante's sidestepping of both Aristotle and the Thomist tradition. Because, as Lefort emphasizes in his essay, unlike Aristotle, Dante does not limit himself to imagining a restricted community, defined by a delimited space, whose limited character would enable precisely the expression of what is in fact Aristotle's real question: the organization of the natural sociability of human beings. For Dante, not only is there no limitation but there can be no such limitation, precisely because the human race includes, as Lefort explains, 'nations of different sizes, peoples who do not know each other, who are exposed to different climates and attached to their particular customs, and whose unity rests on their common submission to the jurisdiction of a monarch'.[13] Lefort goes on to quote the following passage from Book I of the *Monarchia*:

> whatever constitutes the purpose of the civil society of the human race [...] will be here the first principle, in terms of which all subsequent propositions to be proved will be demonstrated with sufficient rigour; for it would be foolish to suppose that there is one purpose for this society and another for that, and not a common purpose for all of them.[14]

The overlaying of *humanitas* and *civilitas* is clear here, and immediately redefines what we are to understand by universality; the universal end or cause, so Lefort informs us, is that of humanity understood as *all human beings together*. Universal society is no longer exclusively that of

---

13   Lefort, 'Dante's Modernity', p. 6.
14   Dante Alighieri, *Monarchy*, ed. and trans. by Prue Shaw (Cambridge: Cambridge University Press, 1996), p. 5 (I, ii, 8 [translation amended]). [Translator's note: All quotations throughout are taken from this translation, which is now also available online at <https://www.danteonline.it/monarchia> [accessed 5 December 2019]. Among the material of this website devoted to the *Monarchia* is the Latin text of Shaw's critical edition: Dante Alighieri, *Monarchia*, ed. by Prue Shaw, Edizione Nazionale delle opere di Dante Alighieri a cura della Società Dantesca Italiana, v (Florence: Le Lettere, 2009).]

the Church, but rather that of unified humanity; it stems, as Gilson had already highlighted in his *Dante the Philosopher*[15] — a text which guides Lefort's commentary a great deal —, from the secularization of the ideal of universal Christendom.

Dante's second sidestep concerns Thomism. "'[T]he necessity which requires humans to communize the resources of their individual reason'"[16] now functions at the level of temporal society, not — or not only — because earthly life is now valued for its own sake, but because it is in this life that the end which is proper to humans can be realized. The *possible intellect* means, as a consequence, the presence and realization of God, who is cause and end, in the interaction between humans themselves. But this communizing of resources is also a form of interaction, because, if humanity has its own end — the actualization of the intellective power —, the individual itself is insufficient, for it is only from the cooperation of all individuals that this actualization can be achieved. Another quotation from Dante:

> And since that potentiality cannot be fully actualized all at once *in any one individual or in any one of the particular social groupings enumerated above,* there must needs be a *multitude* in the human race, through whom the whole of this potentiality can be actualized.[17]

This cooperation between human beings, between nations, between peoples, needs of course to be understood as sub-

---

15   Étienne Gilson, *Dante the Philosopher*, trans. by David Moore (London: Sheed & Ward, 1948).

16   Ibid., p. 166 [translation amended], cited by Lefort, 'Dante's Modernity', p. 5.

17   Dante, *Monarchy*, I, iii, 8. Emphasis added [translation amended].

ject to the condition of unity (the unity of the monarch). But cooperation is itself subject to the constitution of a unitary model, a unity which is rendered by Dante in the form of a body — the multitude representing from this perspective all the *members* of this body. Now, this organic character, to which I will return shortly, allows for a two-fold operation. The figure of the Church as the body of Christ is here replaced by that of the body of humanity whose unity is in God alone (and whose actualization is reliant upon the rule of one alone, the monarch). But the organicity inferred by the image of the body also enables the relationship which is established between the members themselves to be qualified as *cooperation*, in other words, as reciprocal dependency: the necessity for each person, in their *uniqueness*, and directed by one alone (the monarch), to actualize, that is, to constitute along with everyone else, the possible intellect. The concept of the One-body is built on the basis of a bringing together of the singularities of which it is formed — the term 'singularity' is here deliberately 'imported', but I accept the risk —, which means that the disappearance of these singularities is never required. Lefort immediately grasps the importance of this fact: 'Although already present previously, the thought of *the one* proves to be more profound than that of the whole.'[18] Here, the *one* and the *whole* mean entirely different things: no doubt this is what allows us to understand the way in which Lefort will try against all the odds to create a sort of mirror construction of the Dante of the *Monarchia* and of the La Boétie of the *Discourse on Voluntary Servitude*. Indeed, how is it possible not to bring into conflict Dante's assertion that unity (the unity of humanity in God) must be realized under the rule of one alone

---

18   Lefort, 'Dante's Modernity', p. 15.

(the monarch) and La Boétie's obsession with the *Against One*? Perhaps by disconnecting, or by distinguishing, that which relates to *unity* (understood as the articulation of unique ones, as the cooperation of the multitude) from that which relates to the *whole* (understood as the erasure of the unique ones and the reduction to identity). This is what seems to be demonstrated by the analyses which Lefort has devoted to political translations of the dynamics of the whole, from the very start of his intellectual output onwards. For proceeding through *totalization*, asserting the violence which at once covers and reduces the whole also means giving a name, in the modern period which is ours, to the network of totalitarian regimes on which Lefort has worked so extensively.

It is of course necessary to emphasize here, since it is one of the aspects which marks Dante's distancing of himself from Aristotle, the way in which the question of the limitation of the ideal community in space is wholly transformed: the civil society of the human race, universal *civilitas*, knows of no spatial limits. But the same observation also pertains to that other fundamental dimension, history, which much of Book II explores from the days of Rome. For the actualization of the possible intellect also requires a stratification in time: the multitude of members who coexist and cooperate is constituted by a succession of gestures and knowledges, which accumulate slowly. These are quite literally the 'waves' of human activity, whose sedimentation gives birth to human history as the realization of the telos of the human race — a realization which is conceivable only in this history, as a result of sedimentary deposits and successive layers of stratification. In this history, the classical authors have their place, just as Dante has his — and just as we, who read Dante today, probably have our own place too.

Lefort, whose attachment to history I have already sought to highlight at the start of this essay, is particularly attuned to the *thickness of history* (an expression which, for Lefort, in fact comes from Merleau-Ponty) — a thickness which Lefort finds precisely in Dante. Lefort notes: 'Let us recall what Dante says in the *Convivio*: "And all our troubles, if we really search out their origins, derive in some way from not knowing how to use time."'[19] This remark can be read in two ways: on the one hand, we need to read Dante in the same way that Lefort wanted to read Machiavelli, allowing his oeuvre to unfold as *work*, which evidently implies an essential thickness of time; on the other hand, the actualization of the possible intellect requires the participation of all people *throughout time*. It is in this regard that Dante is astonishingly modern: history becomes here the *milieu* in which the affirmation of humankind's humanity (*humanitas*) in its political form (*civilitas*) is conceived. And Lefort himself concludes his own text by exhorting us to know '*how to use time*'.[20]

I announced at the beginning of this essay a second set of questions, which are certainly rooted in Dante's text but which are also largely projected onto it from Lefort's emergent obsession with the critique of the One, in all its forms (we might mention, by way of example, self-identity, society's closing in on itself, the erasure of social conflict, the State-form, party structures, the historical emergence of totalitarian regimes, and so on). If one searches for it

---

19   Ibid., p. 48, citing from Dante Alighieri, *Convivio: A Dual-Language Critical Edition*, ed. and trans. by Andrew Frisardi (Cambridge: Cambridge University Press, 2018), IV, ii, 10.

20   Lefort, 'Dante's Modernity', p. 85.

within the sphere of political thought, the philosophical root of this radical critique is represented for Lefort by the figure of La Boétie, to whom he devotes an essay, in 1976, designed to accompany a new edition of the *Discourse on Voluntary Servitude* — whose full title, we must remember, is the *Discourse on Voluntary Servitude or Against One.* Seventeen years later, when 'Dante's Modernity' is first published in French, it is once more the figure of La Boétie who returns and who comes into tension with the text of the *Monarchia.*

The context of this confrontation is clear, since both texts are in reality a response to one common question: what is the basis for the power of one alone? Of course, the responses of Dante and La Boétie to this question stem from two diametrically opposed points of view. And yet Lefort complicates the play of oppositions, because everything in reality seems to revolve around a different problem: what are we to understand by the word *one*? What does it mean? To what does it refer? Having noted that, according to La Boétie, people, through their desire, and soon their will to servitude, 'give in to the charm of the name of the one alone',[21] some sort of unity must also be recognized amongst humans, without which their common humanity would lose all its consistency. Lefort underscores the difficulty that La Boétie faces: humans have something in common, but they are also 'irreducibly distinct'.[22] Humanity is one, but how are we to understand this unity without relating it immediately to the power of one alone? And even before that: how are we to maintain the singularities which constitute it? The answer given by the *Discourse* rests on a sort of reworking of the notion of

---

21   Ibid., p. 80.
22   Ibid., p. 81.

a *mould*. There is one *same* mould from which all people are fashioned, because Nature placed in each of them a common ground, which La Boétie explains as follows:

> Hence, since this kind mother has given us the whole world as a dwelling place, has lodged us in the same house, has fashioned us according to the same model so that in beholding one another we might almost recognize ourselves; since she has bestowed upon us all the great gift of voice and speech for fraternal relationship, thus achieving by the common and mutual statement of our thoughts a communion of our wills [...].[23]

The common is, in other words, the extraordinary possibility of affirming at the same time the *communion* and the *differences*. Each singularity does not negate the possibility of recognizing the other (precisely because what we have in common is that we are absolutely singular; the common is, here, that of the difference that each of us irreducibly represents); language, which we share, accordingly makes the expression of different voices possible, which in turn also makes possible the communion of wills. Humanity is indeed *one*, but this unity is only conceivable to the extent that it immediately implies the interrelationship between the irreducible singularities that we are. Lefort therefore comments:

> The visible sign of union is deceptive: in truth, nature has made us *not so much united [unis] as all ones [uns]*. However, individuals only discover themselves as ones [uns] *through the relationship* with those with whom they share their life.[24]

---

23 Étienne de La Boétie, *Anti-Dictator: The 'Discours sur la servitude volontaire' of Étienne de La Boétie, Rendered into English*, trans. by Harry Kurz (New York: Columbia University Press, 1942), p. 14.

24 Lefort, 'Dante's Modernity', pp. 81–82. Emphasis added.

In the essay which Lefort devotes in 1976 to La Boétie, an essay whose title is in and of itself a declaration of open war — 'The name of the One' (the One has, in Lefort, gained its capital letter: it is clearly the enemy) —, things are even clearer, and it is important to highlight at least two aspects of that analysis, since they prefigure in a troubling way the commentary on Dante's text which concerns us here.

The opposition, which also recurs in Lefort's 1993 essay, between being *united* (that is, constituting *One*, under the rule of one alone) and being *ones* [*uns*] (in the plural) is already present, and is even put forward in a set and radicalized form. First of all, in a negative manner, because it is not enough to imagine, in front of the One, an other, in a way *its Other*, nor can the problem be solved by setting society in front of the power of the One (the power of one alone). Thinking that society can be a sort of counterbalance to the One can only mean one thing: that our understanding of society 'is embodied as the One, that the plural, denying itself, is swallowed up in the One'.[25] Here there is the danger of that closing in on itself of the social which can make it reproduce in a specular fashion what it had in contrast thought to oppose, whereas it ends up merely imitating those characteristics. Lefort knows well that the logic of the One is not only tenacious but also insidious: 'a tenacious illusion, it is true, from which it is perhaps impossible to free oneself entirely, since in the end it is difficult not to talk about the People, and to resort *to a name which is attractive*

25　Claude Lefort, 'Le Nom d'Un', in Étienne de La Boétie, *Le Discours de la servitude volontaire*, ed. by Pierre Léonard, intro. by Miguel Abensour and Marcel Gauchet, accompanying essays by Pierre Clastres and Claude Lefort, with additional texts by Félicité Lamennais, Pierre Leroux, Auguste Vermorel, Gustav Landauer, and Simone Weil (Paris: Payot, 1976), pp. 247–307 (p. 292).

in it being in the singular.[26] Perhaps we should remember this warning more often today, and ask ourselves what are, today, all the 'names which are attractive in their being in the singular' and which structure our own relation to the political.

But the radicalization of Lefort's position is also positive, and it goes back to the question of the common mould of humans — to their *common* humanity —, and specifically to the question of language. The 'same mould', the 'same form', do not mean, in La Boétie, something like an identity of human nature which would in advance reduce any possibility of difference. On the contrary, it is the *common capacity for differences* (which is what each of us is) to create connections and to communicate — returning to Dante for a moment, to *cooperate* — which constitutes here the common of human beings.

The theme of concord is essential here, and it is no doubt one of the obvious connecting points between Dante and La Boétie. Dante in fact writes in a surprising passage:

> It is clear then that everything which is good is good for this reason: that it constitutes a unity. And since concord, in itself, is a good, it is clear that it consists in some unity as in its root. What this root is will appear if we consider the nature or meaning of concord, for concord is the uniform movement of several wills.[27]

Of course, it is possible to turn these lines into a commentary celebrating the one as what is good, and pull Dante towards what in fact the title that he himself gave to his text

---

26   Ibid., p. 293.
27   Dante, *Monarchy*, I, xv, 4–5.

already signals: the power of one alone, the One as principle and commandment — literally, monarchy. But if, as Dante also indicates in this same passage, the condition of possibility of this unity of wills is placed in what is the cause and end of humanity — the realization of the possible intellect —, in this case concord becomes the measured and harmonious cooperation of wills in all their differences in the interaction assumed by that concord. Here we come close to La Boétie's analyses: concord is that which must be constructed by interrelating differences, in *a making,* in a set of practices which literally produce the common. Concord is not the foundation of human relationships but rather the effect of their constantly shifting interactions.

Lefort, in a wonderful page of his 1976 essay, lingers in particular over one specific sentence of the *Discourse.* This sentence is the same one that he will return to in 1993 in his commentary on the *Monarchia.* We have indeed received, as he recalls repeating La Boétie, 'the great gift of voice and speech for fraternal relationship, thus achieving by the common and mutual statement of our thoughts a communion of our wills'.[28] Lefort then comments:

> In fact, thinking about the fact of language, we are already thinking about the separation and the bringing together of subjects, we are already thinking about the enigmatic event of freedom, which supposes along with the mutual declaration of thoughts to each other the moment of a will to speak whose conditions cannot be found in an earlier state, and whose origin is to be found neither in individuals, since it is in order to speak that they are ones [*uns*], nor outside of them, since it is with and through each other that they speak. Thinking language means already thinking

---

28　La Boétie, *Anti-Dictator,* p. 14.

> the political, freed from the Illusion of the One. For asserting that the destiny of humans is to be not all united [*unis*] but *all ones* [*uns*] means reducing the social relationship to communication and the reciprocal expression of agents, mutually welcoming on principle the differences, arguing that difference is not reducible except in the imaginary and, at the same time — let us not forget to note this —, denouncing the falsehood of those in power who claim that the union of their subjects or of their citizens is the sign of the good society.[29]

But then, without unity, are we doomed to discord? We know Lefort's answer: to admit that the interplay of differences, that conflictuality, what he will call the 'original division of the social', all amount to discord would be to forget what we have learnt from Machiavelli, from La Boétie, and no doubt also from Marx (if we do not reduce him to what orthodox Marxism has made of him) — and even from Spinoza, on whom, however, Lefort never worked.

The question then becomes: where does Dante belong in this genealogy? The power and the beauty of the 1993 commentary stem precisely from the wager that Lefort makes in this regard — it is tempting to add, against the very evidence of Dante's text. But we know, as Lefort reminds us, that reading is misreading, that reading is transformative, and that reading means taking charge. Misreading, transformation, and taking charge do not occur, however, without proper foundations: there is indeed an element on the basis of which turning Dante against himself, or redefining the unity of the *possible intellect* as the *common of differences* and as the cooperation of the *ones*, can indeed be upheld. This aspect is present in La

---

29   Lefort, 'Le nom d'Un', p. 292.

Boétie, as well as in Dante, and it is precisely what Lefort aptly perceives. It is fraternity. In *The Discourse*, La Boétie speaks about 'fraternal affection'. Dante, in the *Monarchia*, declares: "'Behold how good and how pleasant it is for *brethren to dwell together in unity* [*habitare fratres in unum*].'"[30]

What ends up emerging, as a result of this strange diagonal line connecting fourteenth-century Florence and sixteenth-century France, is that fraternity is the name of that which escapes the individual and the One, that fraternity is the necessary third party between the *freedom of the ones* and the *equality of all* which is at once the promise and the guarantee of the common as a cooperation of singularities.

Perhaps, then, if we remember Dante's modernity and if we pin our colours to that mast, if we make this fraternity which unites us without erasing each of our singularities our very own, the realization of a *civilitas* worthy of the *humanitas* which we share becomes conceivable.

TRANSLATED FROM THE FRENCH BY
JENNIFER RUSHWORTH

---

30   Dante, *Monarchy*, I, xvi, 5, citing here from Psalm 132, v. 1 according to the Vulgate numbering, or Psalm 133, v. 1, in the Authorized Version. Emphasis added.

References

Alighieri, Dante, *Convivio: A Dual-Language Critical Edition*, ed. and trans. by Andrew Frisardi (Cambridge: Cambridge University Press, 2018)

—— 'Epistola X: To Can Grande della Scala', in Dante Alighieri, *Epistolae: The Letters of Dante*, ed. and trans. by Paget Toynbee (Oxford: Clarendon, 1920), pp. 160–211

—— *Monarchia*, ed. by Prue Shaw, Edizione Nazionale delle opere di Dante Alighieri a cura della Società Dantesca Italiana, v (Florence: Le Lettere, 2009), Latin text also available online, <http://www.danteonline.it/monarchia> [accessed 5 December 2019]

—— *Monarchy*, ed. and trans. by Prue Shaw (Cambridge: Cambridge University Press, 1996), text also available online, <https://www.danteonline.it/monarchia> [accessed 5 December 2019]

Ascoli, Albert Russell, *Dante and the Making of a Modern Author* (Cambridge: Cambridge University Press, 2008) <https://doi.org/10.1017/CBO9780511485718>

Baron, Hans, *The Crisis of the Early Italian Renaissance*, 2nd, rev. edn (Princeton, NJ: Princeton University Press, 1966)

Dadot, Pierre, and Christian Laval, *Commun: Essai sur la révolution au XXIe siècle* (Paris: La Découverte, 2014), English as *Common: On Revolution in the 21st Century* (London: Bloomsbury, 2019)

Gilson, Étienne, *Dante the Philosopher*, trans. by David Moore (London: Sheed & Ward, 1948)

Hardt, Michael, and Antonio Negri, *Commonwealth* (Cambridge, MA: Belknap, 2009) <https://doi.org/10.2307/j.ctvjsf48h>

—— *Multitude: War and Democracy in the Age of Empire* (New York, NY: The Penguin Press, 2004)

Hartog, François, *Regimes of Historicity: Presentism and Experiences of Time*, trans. by Saskia Brown (New York: Columbia University Press, 2015) <https://doi.org/10.7312/columbia/9780231163767.001.0001>

Homer, *Iliad*, ed. and trans. by A. T. Murray, rev. by William F. Wyatt, 2 vols, Loeb Classical Library, 170 (Cambridge, MA: Harvard University Press, 1999)

Howard, Dick, *The Specter of Democracy* (New York: Columbia University Press, 2002)

Kantorowicz, Ernst H., *The King's Two Bodies: A Study in Mediaeval Political Theology* (Princeton, NJ: Princeton University Press, 1997)

La Boétie, Étienne de, *Anti-Dictator: The 'Discours sur la servitude volontaire' of Étienne de La Boétie, Rendered into English*, trans. by Harry Kurz (New York: Columbia University Press, 1942)

—— *Mémoire sur la pacification des troubles*, ed. by Malcolm Smith (Geneva: Droz, 1983)

Laval, Christian, Pierre Sauvêtre, and Ferhat Taylan, eds, *L'Alternative du commun* (Paris: Hermann, 2019)

Lefort, Claude, 'La Cité des vivants et des morts', in Jules Michelet, *La Cité des vivants et des morts. Préfaces et Introductions* (Paris: Belin, 2002), pp. 5–65

—— *Essais sur le politique, XIXe–XXe siècles* (Paris: Seuil, 1986), English as *Democracy and Political Theory*, trans. by David Macey (Cambridge: Polity, 1988)

—— 'Le Nom d'Un', in Étienne de La Boétie, *Le Discours de la servitude volontaire*, ed. by Pierre Léonard, intro. by Miguel Abensour and Marcel Gauchet, accompanying essays by Pierre Clastres and Claude Lefort, with additional texts by Félicité Lamennais, Pierre Leroux, Auguste Vermorel, Gustav Landauer, and Simone Weil (Paris: Payot, 1976), pp. 247–307

—— *Le Travail de l'œuvre Machiavel* (Paris: Gallimard, 1972), partially translated into English as *Machiavelli in the Making*, trans. by Michael B. Smith (Evanston, IL: Northwestern University Press, 2012)

—— 'Maintenant', *Libre*, 1 (1977), pp. 3–28, English as 'Then and Now', trans. by Dick Howard, Jean Cohen, Patricia Tummons, Mark Poster, and Andrew Arato, *Telos: A Quarterly Journal of Radical Thought*, 36 (1978), pp. 29–42 <https://doi.org/10.3817/0678036029>

—— 'La Modernité de Dante', in Dante, *La Monarchie*, trans. by Michèle Gally (Paris: Belin, 1993), pp. 6–76

—— 'La Nation élue et le rêve de l'empire universel', in *L'Idée d'humanité. Données et Débats, actes du XXXIVe Colloque des intellectuels juifs de la langue française*, ed. by Jean Halpérin and Georges Lévitte (Paris: Albin Michel, 1995), pp. 97–112

—— 'Préface', in Alexis de Tocqueville, *Souvenirs*, ed. by Luc Monnier, with notes by J. P. Mayer and B. M. Wicks-Boisson (Paris: Gallimard, 1999), pp. i–l

—— *Écrire. À l'épreuve du politique* (Paris: Calmann-Lévy, 1992), English as *Writing: The Political Test*, trans. and ed. by David Ames Curtis (Durham, NC: Duke University Press, 2000)

—— *Éléments d'une critique de la bureaucratie* (Geneva: Droz, 1971), a small selection of essays translated into English as part of Claude Lefort, *The Political Forms of Modern Society: Bureaucracy, Democracy, Totalitarianism*, ed. and intro. by John B. Thompson, trans. by Alan Sheridan, Terry Karten, and John B. Thompson (Cambridge: Polity, 1986), pp. 29–136

Lubac, Henri de, *Exégèse médiévale: les quatre sens de l'Écriture*, 2 vols in 4 (Paris: Aubier, 1959–64)

—— *Medieval Exegesis: The Four Senses of Scripture*, trans. by Mark Sebanc and E. M. Macierowski, 3 vols (Grand Rapids, MI: Eerdmans, 1998–2009)

Machiavelli, Niccolò, *The Discourses*, ed. by Bernard Crick, trans. by Leslie J. Walker, rev. by Brian Richardson (London: Penguin, 2013)

Michelet, Jules, *History of the French Revolution*, ed. by Gordon Wright, trans. by Charles Cocks (Chicago, IL: University of Chicago Press, 1967)

—— 'Introduction to World History (1831)', trans. by Flora Kimmich, in *On History: Introduction to World History (1831); Opening Address at the Faculty of Letters, 9 January 1834; Preface to the History of France (1869)*, trans. by Flora Kimmich, Lionel Gossman, and Edward K. Kaplan (Cambridge: Open Book Publishers, 2013), pp. 23–118 <https://doi.org/10.11647/OBP.0036.03>

Pocock, J. G. A., *The Machiavellian Moment: Florentine Political Thought and the Atlantic Republican Tradition* (Princeton, NJ: Princeton University Press, 1975)

Revel, Judith, and Antonio Negri, 'Inventer le commun des hommes', *Multitudes*, 31.4 (2007), pp. 5–10 <https:

//doi.org/10.3917/mult.031.0005>; English as 'Inventing the Common', transl. by N. Lavey (2008) <http://www.generation-online.org/p/fp_revel5.htm> [accessed 8 December 2019]

Salutati, Coluccio, 'Letters in Defence of Liberal Studies', in Ephraim Emerton, *Humanism and Tyranny: Studies in the Italian Trecento* (Cambridge, MA: Harvard University Press, 1925), pp. 285–377 <https://doi.org/10.4159/harvard.9780674333178>

Seneca, *Epistles*, trans. by Richard M. Gunmere, 3 vols (Cambridge, MA: Harvard University Press, 1996–2001)

Walzer, Michael, *The Revolution of the Saints: A Study in the Origins of Radical Politics* (Cambridge, MA: Harvard University Press, 1982)

Yates, Frances A., *Astraea: The Imperial Theme in the Sixteenth Century* (London: Routledge & Kegan Paul, 1975)

Notes on the Contributors

Christiane Frey, associate professor of German with an affiliation in Medieval and Renaissance Studies at New York University until 2017, is currently fellow of the Alexander von Humboldt-Foundation at the Humboldt-Universität zu Berlin. Her recent books include *Laune: Poetiken der Selbstsorge von Montaigne bis Tieck* (2016) and the co-edited volumes *Noch einmal anders: Zu einer Poetik des Seriellen* (2016) and *Säkularisierung: Grundlagentexte zur Theoriegeschichte* (2020).

Manuele Gragnolati is professor of Italian literature at Sorbonne Université, associate director of the ICI Berlin, and senior research fellow at Somerville College, Oxford. He is the author of *Experiencing the Afterlife: Soul and Body in Dante and Medieval Culture* (2005) and *Amor che move. Linguaggio del corpo e forma del desiderio in Dante, Pasolini and Morante* (2013), and the co-editor of several volumes on Dante and medieval culture, including the forthcoming *Oxford Handbook of Dante*.

Christoph F. E. Holzhey is the founding director of the ICI Berlin Institute for Cultural Inquiry, which he has led since 2007. He received a PhD in theoretical physics and another one in German literature. He has run several projects at the ICI Berlin and (co-)edited several volumes, among them *The Scandal of Self-Contradiction: Pasolini's Multistable Subjectivities, Traditions, Geographies* (2012); *Multistable Figures: On the Critical Potentials of Ir/Reversible Aspect-seeing* (2014); *De/Constituting Wholes* (2017); and *Re-: An Errant Glossary* (2019).

Claude Lefort (1924–2010) was one of the most prominent French political philosophers of the twentieth century. An early critic of French post-war Marxist orthodoxy from within the Left, Lefort became known internationally for his commitment to radical democracy and his trenchant insights into the totalitarian threats of the twentieth century. He taught at the École des Hautes Études en Sciences Sociales (EHESS) and the Centre de recherches politiques Raymond Aron in Paris. Among his most important publications are *Le Travail de l'œuvre Machiavel* (1972); *Les Formes de l'histoire* (1978); *Essais sur le politique: XIXe et XXe siècles* (1986); *Le Temps présent* (2007).

Judith Revel is professor of contemporary philosophy at Paris Nanterre University. She works mainly on the thought of the political and representations of history in France and Italy after 1945. Member of the Centre Michel Foucault, of the scientific council of the Institut Mémoires de l'édition contemporaine (IMEC) and of the scientific committee of the Collège International de Philosophie, she is also assistant director of the Sophiapol Laboratory (Sociology, philosophy and political anthropology).

Jennifer Rushworth is lecturer in French and comparative literature at University College London, having previously been a Junior Research Fellow at St John's College, Oxford. She is the author of two books, *Discourses of Mourning in Dante, Petrarch, and Proust* (2016) and *Petrarch and the Literary Culture of Nineteenth-Century France* (2017).

Arnd Wedemeyer is senior researcher at the ICI Berlin. He earned his PhD from the Humanities Center at Johns Hopkins University, and has taught at Princeton and Duke University. His research focuses on political and continental philosophy, comparative literature, and art and cultural history. He has published on Kant, Kafka, Jacob Taubes and Carl Schmitt, Borges and Salomo Friedländer, and Joseph Beuys. He has co-edited *Re-: An Errant Glossary* (2019).

Cultural Inquiry

EDITED BY CHRISTOPH F. E. HOLZHEY
AND MANUELE GRAGNOLATI

Vol. 1   TENSION/SPANNUNG
          Edited by Christoph F. E. Holzhey

Vol. 2   METAMORPHOSING DANTE
          Appropriations, Manipulations, and Rewritings in
          the Twentieth and Twenty-First Centuries
          Edited by Manuele Gragnolati, Fabio Camilletti,
          and Fabian Lampart

Vol. 3   PHANTASMATA
          Techniken des Unheimlichen
          Edited by Fabio Camilletti, Martin Doll, and
          Rupert Gaderer

Vol. 4   Boris Groys / Vittorio Hösle
          DIE VERNUNFT AN DIE MACHT
          Edited by Luca Di Blasi and Marc Jongen

Vol. 5   SARA FORTUNA
          WITTGENSTEINS PHILOSOPHIE DES
          KIPPBILDS
          Aspektwechsel, Ethik, Sprache

Vol. 6   THE SCANDAL OF SELF-CONTRADICTION
          Pasolini's Multistable Subjectivities, Geographies,
          Traditions
          Edited by Luca Di Blasi, Manuele Gragnolati, and
          Christoph F. E. Holzhey

Vol. 7   SITUIERTES WISSEN UND REGIONALE
          EPISTEMOLOGIE
          Zur Aktualität Georges Canguilhems und Donna J.
          Haraways
          Edited by Astrid Deuber-Mankowsky and
          Christoph F. E. Holzhey

Vol. 8   MULTISTABLE FIGURES
On the Critical Potentials of Ir/Reversible
Aspect-Seeing
Edited by Christoph F. E. Holzhey

Vol. 9   Wendy Brown / Rainer Forst
THE POWER OF TOLERANCE
Edited by Luca Di Blasi and Christoph F. E.
Holzhey

Vol. 10   DENKWEISEN DES SPIELS
Medienphilosophische Annäherungen
Edited by Astrid Deuber-Mankowsky and Reinhold
Görling

Vol. 11   DE/CONSTITUTING WHOLES
Towards Partiality Without Parts
Edited by Manuele Gragnolati and Christoph F.E.
Holzhey

Vol. 12   CONATUS UND LEBENSNOT
Schlüsselbegriffe der Medienanthropologie
Edited by Astrid Deuber-Mankowsky and Anna
Tuschling

Vol. 13   AURA UND EXPERIMENT
Naturwissenschaft und Technik bei Walter
Benjamin
Edited by Kyung-Ho Cha

Vol. 14   LUCA DI BLASI
DEZENTRIERUNGEN
Beiträge zur Religion der Philosophie im 20.
Jahrhundert

Vol. 15   RE-
An Errant Glossary
Edited by Christoph F. E. Holzhey and Arnd
Wedemeyer

VOL . 16   CLAUDE LEFORT
          DANTE'S MODERNITY
          An Introduction to the Monarchia
          With an Essay by Judith Revel
          Translated from the French by Jennifer Rushworth
          Edited by Christiane Frey, Manuele Gragnolati,
          Christoph F. E. Holzhey, and Arnd Wedemeyer

www.ingramcontent.com/pod-product-compliance
Lightning Source LLC
La Vergne TN
LVHW051542170726
843492LV00006B/1895